The Theory of Collusion and Competition Policy

The Theory of Collusion and Competition Policy

Joseph E. Harrington, Jr.

The MIT Press
Cambridge, Massachusetts
London, England

This book was set in Times Roman by Westchester Publishing Services. Printed and bound in the United States of America.

Library of Congress Cataloging-in-Publication Data

Names: Harrington, Joseph Emmett, 1957– author.
Title: The theory of collusion and competition policy / Joseph E. Harrington, Jr.
Description: Cambridge, MA : The MIT Press, 2017. | Includes bibliographical references and index.
Identifiers: LCCN 2017010722 | ISBN 9780262036931 (hardcover : alk. paper)
Subjects: LCSH: Industrial policy. | Trade regulation. | Price fixing. | Competition. | Antitrust law—Economic aspects.
Classification: LCC HD3612 .H37 2017 | DDC 338.6/04801—dc23
LC record available at https://lccn.loc.gov/2017010722

10 9 8 7 6 5 4 3 2 1

To the memory of my father. For his optimism, his good cheer, his integrity, and his taste for beer.

Contents

Contents

Preface

This book reviews the theory of unlawful collusion, which means there is a competition law and firms are colluding in a manner that violates that law and, if convicted, they will be penalized. The book is designed to bring the reader up to speed on the questions posed, the models constructed, and the results and insight derived, as well as identifying topics in need of research. The intended audience is economics scholars who seek to contribute to our understanding of how unlawful collusion operates and the proper design of competition law and enforcement or those who just want to learn about these topics. Doctoral economics students are particularly welcome, and I encourage them to look for the gaps in the literature that could be the source of a thesis topic.

The reader is presumed to have at least a rudimentary understanding of the theory of collusion grounded in the theory of repeated games. Suitable treatments at the masters level are provided in Tirole (1988) and Motta (2004), while Vives (1999) is at the doctoral level. If, before taking a "ramble through the wilds of economic theory,"[1] the reader would like to have some facts about how cartels are structured and the practices that they deploy, I recommend Harrington (2006) and Marshall and Marx (2012). Marshall and Marx (2012) is an innovative treatment designed for practitioners, both lawyers and economists, though it is also of considerable value to scholars. Harrington (2006) is well suited for those seeking institutional and factual grounding before venturing into the theory of collusion in that its coverage of collusive practices is organized around the primary theoretical constructs.

I acknowledge the comments of an anonymous referee, participants at the Legal and Illegal Cartels Conference (ZEW, Mannheim, December 2015), where a preliminary version of this book was presented as a keynote address, and the National Science Foundation (SES-1148129) for financial support.

1 Introduction

1.1 Defining Collusion

Collusion is when firms in a market *coordinate* their behavior for the purpose of producing a *supracompetitive outcome*. A supracompetitive outcome is one in which price exceeds the price that would have occurred without the coordination among firms. In the economic theory of collusion, coordination is with respect to the strategies that firms use. A firm's strategy prescribes its behavior (e.g., what price to set, how much to produce), and that behavior can be contingent on what has transpired in the market (e.g., the prices that firms recently charged) as well as on current market conditions (e.g., a firm's cost and the strength of market demand). In laymen's terms, the definition of collusion put forth by economic theory is:

Collusion is when firms use history-dependent strategies to sustain supracompetitive outcomes through a reward-punishment scheme that rewards a firm for abiding by the supracompetitive outcome and punishes it for departing from it.

If a firm abides by the collusive outcome—which could involve high prices, exclusive territories, customer allocation, and so forth—then it is *rewarded* in the future by rival firms continuing to abide by the collusive outcome (e.g., persisting with high prices); while if it departs from the collusive outcome (e.g., setting a low price, selling above its quota, serving another firm's customers) then it is *punished* in the future by rival firms acting aggressively to reduce the deviating firm's profits (e.g., lowering prices, selling to the deviating firm's customers). Collusion involves an implicit or explicit understanding among firms that ties future rewards and punishments to current behavior and, by doing so, is able to induce compliance with regard to the supracompetitive outcome. This understanding can be viewed as contractual, though the penalties for acting contrary to the terms of the contract take the form of rival firms' future (disciplining) behavior. For this arrangement to be effective, it must be *self-enforcing*, which means that each firm finds it in its best interest to abide by the arrangement as long as all other firms are expected to do so.

A collusive strategy comprises three fundamental elements. First, it describes the *collusive outcome*, such as what common price is to be charged or which firm is to serve which geographic area (when the scheme involves exclusive territories). Second, it describes the *monitoring protocol*; that is, how firms will monitor one another for compliance with the collusive outcome. If prices are observable and the collusive outcome is to set a common high price, then monitoring could be in terms of past prices. However, if the firms supply an intermediate good to industrial buyers (e.g., cement suppliers selling to construction companies) where price can be privately negotiated between a seller and a buyer, then price monitoring will not work. In that case, the supracompetitive outcome could involve an allocation of sales quotas (along with a common price to be set), with monitoring taking the form of comparing realized sales to those sales quotas. Third, the collusive strategy describes the *punishment* that occurs when there is evidence of noncompliance. Among other possibilities, the punishment could be a temporary or permanent reversion to pricing competitively, or it could be a focused price war that has firms charge low prices for the customers of the firm that apparently deviated.

Let us now state more formally, in the jargon of game theory, the meaning of "firms in a market coordinate their behavior for the purpose of producing a supracompetitive outcome." As the competitive benchmark is typically defined to be a Nash equilibrium outcome for some static oligopoly game, a supracompetitive outcome involves higher prices than for a static Nash equilibrium. Coordination on a collusive strategy in a game-theoretic framework is taken to be a subgame perfect (or sequential) equilibrium in a repeated game (where the stage game is the original static oligopoly game), which produces supracompetitive outcomes through the use of history-dependent strategies. More specifically, an outcome with higher prices and profits is sustained by the threat that noncompliance with that outcome (or evidence consistent with noncompliance) is punished with a low continuation payoff, such as a temporary or permanent reversion to a stage game Nash equilibrium, or a finite number of periods with low prices and subsequent return to prices exceeding static Nash equilibrium prices.[1]

Thus far we have defined collusion. However, the focus of this survey is not broadly on collusion but rather on collusion that runs afoul of competition law, which leads us to ask: What is *unlawful* collusion? The answer depends on the particular law, the manner in which the law is interpreted (typically, by the courts), and the evidence that is required for determining when the law has been violated. As liability and evidentiary standards vary across time and space, I will attempt to provide a broadly applicable (but not universal) definition of unlawful collusion.

Competition law as it pertains to prohibiting collusion is generally dated from the Sherman Act in the United States in 1890 (though, in fact, Canada preempted the United States by instituting its competition law in 1889). Section 1 prohibits contracts, combinations, and conspiracies that unreasonably restrain trade.[2] Subsequent judicial rulings have effectively replaced the reference to "contracts, combinations, and conspiracies" with the concept of "agreement." It is now understood that firms are in violation of Section 1 when there is *an agreement among competitors to limit competition*. Though the term "agreement," which is now so integral to defining liability, does not appear in the Sherman Act, many jurisdictions that arrived later to the enforcement game have put the term into their competition law. For example, in the European Union, Article 101 (1) of the TFEU (1999) states: "The following shall be prohibited: all agreements between undertakings, decisions by associations of undertakings and concerted practices which . . . have as their object or effect the prevention, restriction or distortion of competition."

Our question "What is unlawful collusion?" has then become: "What is an agreement to limit competition?" Key judicial decisions by the U.S. Supreme Court have resulted in the interpretation that an agreement resides in a mutual understanding among firms to constrain competition. There is an agreement when firms have a "unity of purpose or a common design and understanding, or a meeting of minds"[3] or "a conscious commitment to a common scheme designed to achieve an unlawful objective."[4] This perspective has been echoed by the European Union's General Court, which has defined an agreement as or as requiring "joint intention"[5] or a "concurrence of wills."[6]

Reference to "meeting of minds," "conscious commitment to a common scheme," and "concurrence of wills" all focus on the same condition: There is a common understanding among firms that they will restrict competition in some fashion. The parallel between conditions on firms' mutual beliefs and the notion of equilibrium has been noted in Yao and DeSanti (1993), Werden (2004), and Kaplow (2013):

Analysis of one-shot games provides the clear definition of self-interest necessary to allow evidence of action against self-interest to play a useful role in inferring the existence of an agreement. If there is a unique Nash, non-cooperative equilibrium to a particular game, as there is in conventional one-shot game oligopoly models, it follows that there is a unique action each player will take if [it] does not coordinate its actions with its rivals. These equilibrium actions are consistent with self-interest, and any other actions are not. . . . The existence of an agreement can be inferred from actions inconsistent with Nash, non-cooperative equilibrium in a one-shot game oligopoly model, even though they are consistent with Nash, non-cooperative equilibrium in an infinitely-repeated oligopoly game.[7]

Though these statements seem to make clear that mutual understanding to constrain competition is unlawful, the U.S. Supreme Court has been equally clear that more is required to draw such a conclusion. In particular, mutual understanding obtained through "shared economic interests" without some overt effort on the part of firms to create that mutual understanding is not in violation of Section 1 of the Sherman Act.

Courts have noted that the Sherman Act prohibits *agreements*, and they have almost uniformly held, at least in the pricing area, that such individual pricing decisions (even when each firm rests its own decisions upon its belief that competitors do the same) do *not* constitute an unlawful agreement under section 1 of the Sherman Act... [T]hat is not because such pricing is desirable (it is not), but because it is close to impossible to devise a judicially enforceable remedy for "interdependent" pricing. How does one order a firm to set its prices *without regard* to the likely reactions of its competitors?[8]

The court has gone on to require that firms have engaged in some expression of intent that results in reliance among themselves to coordinate to reduce competition. An agreement is not just a mutual understanding among firms to engage in coordinated suppression of competition but also an expression of that mutual understanding through the process of its creation:

By operationalizing the idea of an agreement, antitrust law clarified that the idea of an agreement describes a process that firms engage in, not merely the outcome that they reach. Not every parallel pricing outcome constitutes an agreement because not every such outcome was reached through the process to which the law objects: a negotiation that concludes when the firms convey mutual assurances that the understanding they reached will be carried out.[9]

In practice, firms must not only have mutual beliefs to restrain competition but those beliefs must have been achieved through some form of communication.

This legal approach has led to the recognition of three categories of collusion: (1) explicit collusion, (2) tacit collusion, and (3) conscious parallelism. If, for example, firms (or, more to the point, their representatives) reach a mutual understanding by speaking to each other regarding a plan to raise prices, then they have engaged in *explicit* collusion. Explicit collusion involves "easily observable proof that the defendants have exchanged assurances that they will pursue a common course of action."[10] In contrast, if, for example, a firm announces its plan to raise prices at an industry gathering, which, without any further communication, leads to mutual beliefs that all will raise their prices (as evidenced by subsequent behavior), then they have engaged in *tacit* collusion. Tacit collusion does not entail an express exchange of assurances but does require firms communicate "their intent to raise prices and their reliance on one another to do the same."[11] And if, for example, a firm raises its price and other firms match that price and there is no communication, that is an example of conscious parallelism, which is a process "not in itself unlawful, by which firms in a concentrated market might in effect share monopoly power, setting their prices at a profit-maximizing, supracompetitive level by recognizing their shared economic interests."[12]

It should be clear from the preceding discussion that economic (or, equivalently, game-theoretic) collusion and unlawful collusion are distinct objects. Economic collusion focuses on firms' outcomes and how those outcomes are supported by mutual beliefs with regard to firms' strategies. In short, economic collusion focuses on the equilibrium. In contrast, unlawful collusion is also concerned with how the collusive equilibrium came about and thus with the equilibrating process. Economic collusion can be lawful. Putting aside excessive pricing laws,[13] it is lawful to charge supracompetitive prices and to enforce such prices through the implicit threat of a punishment, so long as the threat did not involve any communication. At the same time, unlawful collusion need not be economic collusion. Communicating to coordinate a move from a static Nash equilibrium to a less competitive static Nash equilibrium is unlawful even though it is not a repeated game equilibrium.[14]

Terminological Tangent

Before leaving this topic, let me discuss an abuse of terminology routinely perpetrated by industrial organization economists. The equilibrium approach says: *If* firms have mutual beliefs regarding some collusive strategy profile then, under these conditions, that strategy profile is stable (in the sense of equilibrium) and thus collusion can persist. That approach is predicated on the *presumption of mutual understanding* and thus has nothing to say about *how mutual understanding was achieved*, which is exactly the focus of the law. Because the process by which an equilibrium is reached is not part of (almost) all economic theories of collusion, they cannot then encompass the legal and practical distinction between explicit and tacit collusion that focuses on the process by which firms move from a stage game Nash equilibrium to a collusive equilibrium for a repeated game. Equilibrium theories have nothing to say about the disequilibrium process and, on those grounds, it is not meaningful to refer to an equilibrium theory of collusion as either tacit or explicit, for it is mute on the matter.[15]

Therefore, regardless of the long history of oligopoly theorists referring to their theories as "tacit collusion" (for which I admit mea culpa), such a reference is misleading and unnecessary. It is misleading, because it does not deal with how firms achieved an equilibrium, which is the defining distinction between explicit and tacit collusion. Classifying a theory of collusion as "tacit" will either confuse legal scholars—as they wonder how the model is one of tacit collusion rather than explicit collusion, given that there is no discussion of communication—or worse yet, they will be misled into thinking that the theory is actually pertinent to understanding collusive behavior in the absence of communication.[16] In addition, dropping the term "tacit" will not lose any substance for economists, because it has no formal meaning in a game-theoretic context. There will then will be no confusion among economists if the term "collusion" is used instead of "tacit collusion." For these reasons, I propose that we dispense with the term "tacit" when referring to equilibrium theories of collusion.[17]

1.2 Overview of Book

In this book, I review theoretical research that addresses two broad questions: (1) What is the impact of competition law and enforcement on whether firms collude, how long they collude, and how much they collude? and (2) What is the optimal design of competition law and enforcement? Chapter 3 examines the first question. The second question is addressed in chapter 4 though, along the way, I will cover some research pertinent to the first question. As a starting point, chapter 2 discusses some general issues with regard to taking into account competition law and enforcement in models of collusion. In the context of these two questions, the goal is to describe some canonical models, review some key results and insights, and suggest future lines of inquiry.

Let me conclude this chapter by discussing what is not covered in the book. The focus is on theory, and thus I do not cover experimental and empirical research.[18] In the domain of the theory of collusion, most of the models will have perfect monitoring, because there is very little research that encompasses competition law and enforcement in a model of collusion with imperfect monitoring. While many collusive practices can only be understood in the context of imperfect monitoring, much of the insight delivered thus far regarding the impact of competition law and enforcement is not tied to that feature.

Some of the theoretical literature on collusion and competition policy is also not covered in this survey. It is nearly universal to model the decision-making entity as a profit maximizer and to assume it is the firm that colludes and is penalized. In practice, it is the employees of the firms who collude, and they can be motivated by factors other than profit and be subject to penalties distinct from those levied on the firm. There is some research that encompasses agency issues that I do not cover.[19] This is a critical area for future research. There is also a small literature examining the implications and design of competition policy in the context of auctions. To keep the discussion focused, I limit my attention to product markets but make reference to some relevant research on collusion and competition policy with regard to auctions. Finally, there are some competition policy issues dealing with vertical restraints and collusion which are not reviewed here.[20]

2 Game-Theoretic Modeling Issues

Before looking at some models in detail, this chapter provides a brief description of a few central modeling issues when collusion is unlawful. Formal details regarding how these issues are handled will be discussed in the remainder of the book.

To begin, let us think about the various ways in which to model collusion, prior to inserting into the model competition law along with a competition authority (hereafter, CA) to enforce that law. We start with a static model of oligopoly which typically involves firms simultaneously choosing quantities or prices with either identical or differentiated products. The Nash equilibria of that static oligopoly model comprise the competitive (or noncollusive) benchmark. As we will later find, it is not uncommon to consider a very simple oligopoly model, such as the Prisoners' Dilemma or the Bertrand price game with homogenous goods, to keep the analysis tractable once it is enriched with competition law and enforcement. Of course, when the focus is on how competition policy impacts the collusive price, it is necessary to consider richer oligopoly models.

With that static oligopoly model, collusion can be introduced in two general ways. The static approach is to assume that firms act collectively rather than make independent choices. One common objective is for firms to choose their prices or quantities to maximize joint profits. When firms are symmetric—so that all have the same profit function (which requires identical costs, identical capacities, and either identical or symmetrically differentiated products)—this is a natural objective, as joint profit maximization also means maximizing each firm's profit. However, when firms are not symmetric, joint profit maximization is not a plausible objective (unless side payments are allowed), because it is possible for a firm to earn less profit by colluding than by competing and, more generally, for the returns from collusion to be so unevenly distributed that some firms would most likely be discontent with the arrangement. However, if side payments are permitted, then it is reasonable for firms to coordinate to maximize industry profits, as they can arbitrarily allocate those profits among firms to ensure that all are better off by having formed a cartel. If firms are asymmetric and side payments are not possible, then one could assume that firms' prices and quantities are chosen according to some bargaining solution, such as the Nash Bargaining Solution, where the threat points are the static Nash equilibrium profits (Schmalensee 1987). In this way, all firms will benefit from collusion, and how much they benefit will be the result of negotiation.

The second approach to introducing collusion is both more sound and more common. It entails deriving collusive behavior as an equilibrium for an infinitely or indefinitely repeated game for which the stage game is the original static oligopoly game. While a static approach can characterize a collusive outcome, a dynamic approach can also address the question of when firms are able to collude; that is, when there exists an equilibrium with supracompetitive prices. In assessing the impact of competition policy, one could, in principle, explore its impact on the set of collusive equilibria, but it is more common to engage in an equilibrium selection and investigate its impact on that equilibrium. When firms are symmetric, a natural selection criterion is Pareto efficiency; that is, the best symmetric equilibrium (either among all subgame perfect equilibria or some class of subgame perfect equilibria). When firms are asymmetric, some of the criteria applied to make a selection include that of balanced temptation (Friedman 1977; Bae 1987), joint profit maximization (if side payments are feasible), and the Nash Bargaining

Solution (Harrington 1989, 1991). With the latter approach, the Nash Bargaining Solution is applied to the set of equilibrium payoff vectors rather than to all payoff vectors in order to ensure that any agreement as to firms' payoffs can actually be implemented with a self-enforcing scheme.

Now that we have a model of collusion, the next step is to modify it to take into account competition law and enforcement. This requires addressing three questions. First, what is illegal? That is, what is unlawful collusion? Second, what is the process by which illegality is determined? That is, what are the conditions under which firms are convicted? Third, what are the implications of illegality having been determined? That is, what are the penalties in the event of conviction?

In specifying what is illegal, almost all economic models do not draw the distinction that exists in the law with regard to different categories of collusion, as described in chapter 1. The approach is instead to focus on a particular class of equilibria and presume that acting according to them is unlawful. This book has as its domain all theories of collusion that capture competition law and enforcement in the model by some likelihood of conviction, which results in some penalties and possible change in conduct (e.g., termination of collusion and reversion to a static Nash equilibrium). There are a few papers, however, that do discriminate between collusive equilibria in a substantive way by considering those models that have firms communicating as part of the equilibrium (that is, sending cheap talk messages) and those that do not. That body of work is small and it is an even smaller subset of it that takes into account competition law by assuming that only collusive equilibria with communication are subject to penalties. More research in that vein is desperately needed.

Having assumed that collusion is unlawful, the second question is addressed by modeling the process by which it is determined that firms have violated the law. In principle, this requires passing through three stages: (1) detection, (2) prosecution, and (3) conviction. In practice, detection of suspected collusion can be done by customers (typically, industrial buyers), uninvolved employees (who are acting as whistleblowers), competing firms not involved in the cartel, and the CA. Prosecution is generally done by the CA, though it can also be pursued by customers seeking compensation in those countries that allow private litigation. Conviction depends on evidentiary standards and other processes, such as plea bargaining. In the literature, it is standard not to model these various stages and instead to compress them all into a probability σ that a cartel is discovered, prosecuted, and convicted (i.e., pays penalties). It is often the case that there is a probability of an investigation ω (which encompasses both discovery and prosecution) and then, conditional on an investigation, a probability of conviction ρ, in which case $\sigma = \omega\rho$.

The probability σ could be a fixed scalar applied each period, or it could be a function of firm behavior. In Harrington (2008b), there is some fixed probability ω each period that an investigation occurs and, conditional on an investigation, the probability of conviction ρ is randomly selected, with higher values reflecting a stronger case for the CA. Alternatively, a probability function could be assumed that makes σ a function of firm behavior. The function σ could be an increasing function of the current period's collusive price (Block, Nold, and Sidak 1981) or an increasing function of the price change (Harrington 2004a, 2005).

While research has allowed firms' prices to affect the probability of detection and conviction, it has not explored how practices more broadly influence it. How does the frequency of meetings impact detection? How do public signals between firms influence detection and conviction? How does the form of collusive practices—compare various market allocation schemes—affect the amount of evidence? Competition policy may be valuable not just in deterring collusion but also by causing firms to pursue less effective means of colluding. That firms do not always pursue the most direct methods of communication is testimony to their desire to avoid being convicted; they are trading off less effective collusion for reducing expected penalties.

Thus far, the probability that a cartel is penalized is specified as an exogenous function. A more foundational approach is to make it the product of the choices of the CA or customers regarding effort to discover a cartel, deciding whether to prosecute, and effort exerted to convict. In the static setting, a CA deciding when to optimally prosecute is considered in Besanko and Spulber (1989), LaCasse (1995), Souam (2001), and Schinkel and Tuinstra (2006), while customers decide when to optimally sue in Besanko and Spulber (1990). Related is Harrington and Chen (2006), which has customers act as empiricists who bring cases when pricing behavior is anomalous. Harrington and Chang (2015) considers each of the three stages—detection, prosecution, conviction—by assuming that the probability of discovery is some exogenous probability, the probability of prosecution is a choice variable on the part of the CA regarding what fraction of possible cases to pursue, and the probability of conviction is exogenously decreasing with the CA's caseload. Finally, the probability a cartel is penalized has been endogenized in some models by allowing self-reporting by cartel members in exchange for leniency. In sum, this general approach takes into account how the optimal behavior of a player determines or influences whether an investigation is conducted, a case is prosecuted, or a conviction is achieved.

The third question that needs to be addressed in order to embed competition law and enforcement in a model of collusion is how to specify the penalties associated with conviction. In practice, explicit penalties take the form of corporate penalties (government fines and customer damages) and individual penalties (government fines, debarment, and incarceration). As the literature has largely just considered collusion from the perspective of profit maximization (rather than a managerial perspective), the focus on penalties has been at the corporate level and, therefore, that will be our focus, too.

In practice, an array of penalty formulas has been used. For the European Commission, the fine is sensitive to many factors but, most critically, to cartel duration and revenue during the time of collusion. An alternative approach is to tie the fine to the incremental profit (or consumer loss) from collusion. In Chile and the United States, the fine can be as high as twice the profit gain to cartel members, while it can be treble that amount in Australia and Germany. For customer damages, the conventional practice in the United States is that it equals the number of units sold during the cartel period multiplied by the overcharge, which equals the collusive price minus the but-for price. (This is the price that would have occurred "but for" collusion and is most naturally thought to be a static Nash equilibrium price, but it need not be if firms would have engaged in some legal variety of collusion.) The penalty can be a multiple of damages.

In models of collusive behavior, the approach taken to specify the penalty is typically far simpler than what occurs in practice. It is widely assumed there is a fixed penalty, which, in principle, can depend on market characteristics (perhaps some measures of market size) but is not endogenous to firm behavior. When the penalty is sensitive to firm behavior, the most common assumption is that it depends on firms' prices and quantities in the period that the cartel is caught. The penalty could be increasing in firm revenue or the incremental profit from collusion, or it could use the above-described formula for damages. In addition to these explicit penalties, there is an implicit penalty from conviction, which is the discontinuance of collusion; that is, firms revert to a stage game Nash equilibrium. This reversion may be modeled as permanent or temporary (with the return to collusion occurring after some fixed number of periods or stochastically). It is worth noting that, in practice, collusion could be terminated on detection and prosecution even without a conviction. However, such a possibility is not typically modeled, partly because most models do not draw a distinction between prosecution and conviction.

A significant departure from reality is that most models assume the penalty is based on contemporaneous collusion (that is, collusive prices and quantities in the period in which firms are caught), while penalty formulas actually take into account the cartel's entire lifetime (or at least the part that is documented). In the case of the European Commission, the penalty is proportional to duration. Customer damages in the United States are calculated for all periods for which firms have been found guilty of colluding. While a few papers allow penalties to depend on the cartel's history (Harrington 2004a, 2005, 2014), this dependence introduces a technical challenge, as the game is no longer repeated; there is a state variable in the form of the accumulated penalty from past periods. One approach to allowing penalties to depend on more than contemporaneous collusive effects but without having a state variable is to assume the penalty is proportional to the expected incremental value from colluding; this method is used in Harrington and Chang (2009, 2015). Effectively, it makes the penalty sensitive to the average (equilibrium) impact of the cartel on the present value of profits rather than to the actual impact.

3 Impact of Competition Policy on Collusion

This chapter reviews theoretical research as it pertains to understanding the impact of competition law and enforcement on collusion. Section 3.1 examines how it affects whether a cartel forms and, if one does form, how long the cartel lasts. Given that a cartel forms, section 3.2 looks into how competition law and enforcement influences which firms participate. Finally, section 3.3 discusses how competition law and enforcement impacts the prices set by colluding firms. The Appendix provides a list of notation for easy reference.

3.1 Cartel Formation and Duration

In investigating how competition policy affects whether there is collusion, it is useful to consider how this question is posed in a game-theoretic framework. Most papers do not model cartel formation but instead ask how competition policy affects the conditions for a collusive equilibrium to exist. From that perspective, cartel formation is said to be less likely when the collusive equilibrium conditions are more stringent. If one imagines industries differing in terms of the model's parameters, then a more stringent equilibrium condition translates into a smaller set of industries (that is, a smaller set of parameter constellations) for which collusion is stable (in the sense of being supported by an equilibrium). A very good application of this approach is Chen and Rey (2013). An alternative method is to specify a set of industries and explicitly model the birth and death process of cartels. An attractive feature of those models is that it allows the derivation of average cartel duration and the steady-state presence of cartels. Such a modeling perspective is taken in Harrington and Chang (2009, 2015).

3.1.1 Impact of Competition Policy on the Set of Markets for Which Collusion Is Stable

Let us begin by putting forth a simple model to explore how competition law and enforcement impacts the existence of a collusive equilibrium.[1] Consider an infinitely repeated game in which the stage game is an n-firm Prisoners' Dilemma. Let π^n denote the non-collusive (static Nash equilibrium) per period profit, so the present value of the noncollusive profit stream is $V^n \equiv \pi^n/(1 - \delta)$, where the common discount factor is $\delta \in (0, 1)$. The per period collusive profit is $\pi^c(>\pi^n)$, and suppose that firms sustain collusion using the grim punishment; that is, deviation from the collusive outcome results in permanent reversion to the noncollusive outcome. As long as firms collude, a firm will have a constant profit stream of π^c, which has a present value of $\pi^c/(1 - \delta)$. If a firm deviates from the collusive outcome, it earns profit $\pi^d(>\pi^c)$ in that period and, as a consequence of the grim punishment, π^n thereafter. Thus, in the absence of competition law, collusion is sustainable (that is, the grim trigger strategy is a subgame perfect equilibrium) if and only if

$$\frac{\pi^c}{1 - \delta} \geq \pi^d + \frac{\delta\pi^n}{1 - \delta}.$$

In each period that firms are colluding, there is an exogenous probability $\sigma \in (0, 1)$ that the cartel is discovered, prosecuted, and convicted. In that event, firms are levied a penalty and are assumed not to collude thereafter.[2] The penalty scheme has each firm assessed an amount $f > 0$ for each period the cartel was in place. In principle, if the cartel colluded for T periods prior to conviction then they are liable for a penalty of fT. In practice, the penalty is generally less than that value, because it is based on *documented* cartel duration rather than *true* cartel duration. So as to capture the deterioration of evidence, penalties are assumed to decay. If F^t is the penalty that a firm would have to pay if caught and convicted in period t, it is assumed to evolve as follows: $F^t = \beta F^{t-1} + f$, where $1 - \beta \in (0, 1)$ is the depreciation rate. For technical reasons, it is important for the penalty to depreciate so that it is bounded.

Assuming that, on the equilibrium path, collusion is sustainable in all periods, $V^c(F)$ denotes the collusive value given an accumulated penalty of F. It is defined recursively by

$$V^c(F) = \pi^c + \sigma[\delta V^n - (\beta F + f)] + (1 - \sigma)\delta V^c(\beta F + f), \qquad (3.1)$$

and can be shown to equal

$$V^c(F) = \frac{\pi^c + \sigma\delta V^n}{1 - (1 - \sigma)\delta} - \left(\frac{\sigma\beta[1 - (1 - \sigma)\delta]F + \alpha f}{[1 - (1 - \sigma)\delta\beta][1 - (1 - \sigma)\delta]} \right). \qquad (3.2)$$

The first term is the expected present value of profits from the product market, and the second term is the expected discounted penalty.

Assuming the cartel starts operating in period 1, then $F^0 = 0$ and, on the equilibrium path, $F^t \in [0, f/(1 - \beta)]$, $\forall t \geq 1$, where $f/(1 - \beta)$ is the steady-state penalty. Equilibrium requires that the payoff from colluding, $V^c(F)$, is at least as great as the payoff from deviating. In specifying the deviation payoff, it is assumed that the cartel could be caught in the current period but has no chance of being caught in the future. The equilibrium conditions are then

$$V^c(F) \geq \pi^d + \delta V^n - \sigma(\beta F + f), \ \forall F \in [0, f/(1 - \beta)]. \qquad (3.3)$$

One can show that this equilibrium condition is more stringent when F is higher. Intuitively, given that firms are more likely to end up paying penalties when they continue colluding, deviation (with subsequent cartel breakdown) becomes more attractive as the accumulated penalty grows. As a result, (3.3) holds if and only if it holds for the steady-state penalty of $f/(1 - \beta)$. Setting F equal to $f/(1 - \beta)$ in (3.2), we can solve for the steady-state collusive value:

$$V^c(f/[1 - \beta]) = \frac{\pi^c + \sigma \delta V^n - \sigma(f/[1 - \beta])}{1 - (1 - \sigma)\delta}.$$

Inserting this expression into (3.3) yields the necessary and sufficient condition for collusion to be stable:

$$\frac{\pi^c + \sigma \delta V^n - \sigma(f/[1 - \beta])}{1 - (1 - \sigma)\delta} \geq \pi^d + \delta V^n - \sigma(f/[1 - \beta]). \qquad (3.4)$$

Collusion is said to be deterred if and only if (3.4) does not hold. Of course, if (3.4) holds, then collusion can occur but need not occur; just because an equilibrium with collusion exists does not mean that collusion will occur: there is always an equilibrium without collusion. It is worth noting that collusion can be more profitable than competition—$V^c(f/(1 - \beta)) > V^n$—yet (3.4) is not satisfied. As noted by Buccirossi and Spagnolo (2007), deterrence of cartel formation only requires that competition policy make collusion *unstable*, not unprofitable.

If we consider the Bertrand price game, then $\pi^n = 0$ and $\pi^d = n\pi^c$, in which case (3.4) can be simplified and rearranged to

$$\pi^c \geq \frac{\sigma(1 - \sigma)\delta(f/[1 - \beta])}{n(1 - \sigma)\delta - (n - 1)} \equiv \Psi(\sigma, f, \beta). \qquad (3.5)$$

Suppose industries are identical except for the price of the next best substitute, and that results in variation in the collusive profit π^c. Expression (3.5) says that collusion is possible only in those industries for which $\pi^c \geq \Psi(\sigma, f, \beta)$. The $\Psi(\sigma, f, \beta)$ is larger when competition policy is tougher—as reflected in a higher probability of being caught and convicted σ, a higher penalty f, and more effective documentation of evidence as reflected in a higher β—so more industries are immune to collusion.[3] While both the collusive payoff (on the left-hand side, LHS) and the deviation payoff (on the right-hand side, RHS) in (3.4) are increasing in σ, f, and β, it is straightforward to show that the LHS is more sensitive to the policy parameters—because penalties are more likely to be incurred when firms continue colluding—in which case the equilibrium condition is more stringent.

3.1.2   Impact of Competition Policy on the Cartel Rate

An alternative approach to exploring how competition policy impacts the prevalence of collusion is to explicitly model the birth and death process of cartels. While there is some research that endogenizes cartel formation,[4] the only work that models the birth and death process of cartels is Harrington and Chang (2009, 2015).

Modifying the infinitely repeated n-firm Prisoners' Dilemma, suppose market demand is stochastically realized which produces a potential profit that a firm can earn that is denoted by π. The variable π is independently drawn each period according to the differentiable cdf $H : [\underline{\pi}, \overline{\pi}] \to [0, 1]$, and $\mu \equiv \int_{\underline{\pi}}^{\overline{\pi}} \pi H'(\pi) d\pi$ denotes its finite mean. Collusive profit is equal to that potential profit: $\pi^c = \pi$. As in Rotemberg and Saloner (1986), π is observed prior to firms deciding how to behave. The profit from deviating is $\pi^d = \eta\pi$, where $\eta > 1$, and the noncollusive profit is $\pi^n = \alpha\pi$, where $\alpha \in [0, 1)$.

At any point in time, an industry is either cartelized or not, and moves in and out of the cartel state as follows. Suppose it is currently a cartel. In response to the realization of the profit state π, collusion may not be incentive compatible (i.e., it is not an equilibrium). In that case, the cartel collapses, each firm earns $\alpha\pi$, and the industry shifts to the non-cartel state. If collusion is incentive compatible, then each firms earn π. Whether the cartel collapsed or remained intact, there is a probability σ that the cartel is caught and convicted. If it is convicted, then the industry shifts to the non-cartel state. If instead the industry is not a cartel, then it has a probability $\kappa \in (0, 1)$ of moving to the cartel state.

In modeling a population of industries, the industries are allowed to vary in terms of cartel stability as captured by the parameter η, which controls the amount of profit gained by cheating. The differentiable cdf on industry types is $G : [\underline{\eta}, \overline{\eta}] \to [0, 1]$, where $1 < \underline{\eta} < \overline{\eta}$.

Let V^c denote the firm value in the cartel state and V^{nc} denote the firm value in the non-cartel state. In the event that a cartel is convicted, the penalty levied on a firm is $\gamma([1 - \delta]V^c - \alpha\mu)$, where $\gamma > 0$ and $\alpha\mu$ is average noncollusive profit. This specification allows the penalty to be sensitive to the average incremental gain from colluding. The equilibrium condition is

$$\pi + \delta([1 - \sigma]V^c + \sigma V^{nc}) - \sigma\gamma([1 - \delta]V^c - \alpha\mu)$$
$$\geq \eta\pi + \delta V^{nc} - \sigma\gamma([1 - \delta]V^c - \alpha\mu). \tag{3.6}$$

Noting that the non-cartel value is defined by $V^{nc} = (1 - \kappa)(\alpha\mu + \delta V^{nc}) + \kappa V^c$, one can use it in (3.6) to show that the equilibrium condition holds if and only if

$$\pi \leq \frac{\delta(1 - \sigma)(1 - \kappa)([1 - \delta]V^c - \alpha\mu)}{(\eta - 1)(1 - \delta[1 - \kappa])} \equiv \phi(V^c, \eta). \tag{3.7}$$

Just as in Rotemberg and Saloner (1986), collusion is stable when the profit realization is sufficiently low. When profit is high, the increase in current profit from deviating is large, while the continuation payoff is unaffected (as π is *iid* over time).

The next step is to solve for the equilibrium value for V^c. Given that an industry is cartelized and given that $\pi \leq \phi(V^c, \eta)$, each firm earns collusive profits π. The cartel is caught with probability σ, in which case each firm receives the future payoff V^{nc} less the penalty, and if not caught, then each earns the future collusive value V^c. If instead $\pi > \phi(V^c, \eta)$, then the cartel collapses, so each firm earns $\alpha\pi$ and the future value is V^{nc} less expected penalties. The following equation then defines the implied collusive value,

$\psi(V^c)$, when firms perceive it to be V^c:

$$\psi(V^c, \eta) = \int_{\underline{\pi}}^{\phi(V^c, \eta)} [\pi + \delta((1 - \sigma)V^c + \sigma V^{nc})$$

$$- \sigma\gamma((1 - \delta)V^c - \alpha\mu)]H'(\pi)d\pi$$

$$+ \int_{\phi(V^c, \eta)}^{\overline{\pi}} [\alpha\pi + \delta V^{nc} - \sigma\gamma((1 - \delta)V^c - \alpha\mu)]$$

$$\times H'(\pi)d\pi.$$

A fixed point of ψ is an equilibrium value for V^c. One fixed point is the noncollusive value, $V^c = \alpha\mu/(1 - \delta)$. If σ and γ are sufficiently low, then there is also at least one solution in which firms collude, $V^c > \alpha\mu/(1 - \delta)$. When there are multiple solutions, it is assumed that the maximal solution is selected, and it is denoted by $V^{c*}(\eta)$. The value attached to being in the cartel state, $V^{c*}(\eta)$, is lower when the likelihood of conviction σ is higher, the penalty multiple γ is higher, and the cartel is inherently less stable (i.e., a higher value for η).

Given $V^{c*}(\eta)$, define $\phi^*(\eta)$ as the maximum profit realization such that the cartel is stable: $\phi^*(\eta) \equiv \phi(V^{c*}(\eta), \eta)$ using (3.7). The variable $\phi^*(\eta)$ is a measure of cartel stability, since the cartel is stable if and only if $\pi \le \phi^*(\eta)$. This can be seen more clearly by noting that the probability a cartel survives in any period is $(1 - \sigma)H(\phi^*(\eta))$, which is the probability of the joint event that it is not caught, $1 - \sigma$, and that it does not internally collapse, $H(\phi^*(\eta))$. It can be shown that $(1 - \sigma)H(\phi^*(\eta))$ is increasing in η, so that cartels whose firms have a higher temptation to deviate (higher η) collapse for lower profit states ($\phi^*(\eta)$ is lower) and thus have shorter duration.

At this stage, we can assess the impact of competition policy on the average duration of a cartel. A higher value for σ mechanically means a higher chance that a cartel is shut down because it is caught and convicted. But a higher value for σ (as well as a higher value for γ) also has an indirect effect on cartel duration.

A tougher competition policy lowers the cartel value $V^{c*}(\eta)$, which then makes the cartel less stable, as reflected in a lower profit threshold $\phi^*(\eta)$ at which the cartel collapses, for $\phi^*(\eta)$ is decreasing in σ and γ. Thus, even when a CA does not directly shut down a cartel, it indirectly does so by making internal collapse more likely.

What has been described is a Markov birth and death process for each cartel, from which we can derive a steady-state frequency of cartels. For a continuum of industries of type η, let $C(\eta)$ denote the proportion of cartels among type-η industries. The stationary proportion of type-η industries that are not cartels is defined by

$$1 - C(\eta) = [1 - C(\eta)][(1 - \kappa) + \kappa(1 - H(\phi^*(\eta))) + \kappa H(\phi^*(\eta))\sigma]$$
$$+ C(\eta)[(1 - H(\phi^*(\eta))) + H(\phi^*(\eta))\sigma]. \tag{3.8}$$

Of the $1 - C(\eta)$ industries in the previous period that did not have cartels, a fraction $(1 - \kappa)$ of them are still not cartels (because they did not have the opportunity to cartelize). In addition, a fraction $\kappa(1 - H(\phi^*(\eta)))$ are not cartels because, while they had the opportunity to cartelize, it was not incentive compatible. And finally, a fraction $\kappa H(\phi^*(\eta))\sigma$ are not cartels because, while they had the opportunity to cartelize and it was incentive compatible to do so, they were caught and convicted. Of the $C(\eta)$ industries in the previous period that did have cartels, a fraction $(1 - H(\phi^*(\eta)))$ internally collapsed, and a fraction $H(\phi^*(\eta))\sigma$ did not collapse but were convicted. Solving (3.8) for $C(\eta)$ and aggregating across all industry types, the cartel rate (that is, the fraction of all industries cartelized according to the stationary distribution) is

$$C = \int_{\underline{\eta}}^{\overline{\eta}} C(\eta)G'(\eta)d\eta = \int_{\underline{\eta}}^{\overline{\eta}} \left[\frac{\kappa H(\phi^*(\eta))}{1 - (1 - \sigma - \kappa)H(\phi^*(\eta))} \right] G'(\eta)d\eta.$$

If the penalty rate γ is not too high, then $C > 0$ and C is decreasing in σ.

The attractiveness of this approach is that it explicitly models the birth and death of cartels and thereby is able to assess the impact of competition policy on cartel duration and the frequency of cartels. A harsher competition policy reduces the cartel rate by deterring cartel formation in some industries (that is, expanding the set of industry types for which collusion is never an equilibrium) and reducing cartel duration in other industries (by lowering $\phi^*(\eta)$ and thereby reducing the frequency with which the industry is in the cartel state).

Another deliverable of Harrington and Chang (2009) is providing a way in which to test policy efficacy. It is shown that a rise in the probability of detection and conviction σ causes the immediate collapse of the least stable cartels (that is, those with the highest values of η). This means the surviving cartels are those with lower values of η and thus longer duration. Since this is the pool from which one draws discovered cartels, the average duration of discovered cartels *rises* in the short run in response to a higher value for σ. Inverting this result, consider a policy that is intended to alter the likelihood of detection and conviction, but the question is whether it succeeded (σ rose), is ineffective (σ is unchanged), or is counterproductive (σ fell). What actually happened can be inferred by observing the duration of discovered cartels in the short run. If average cartel duration goes up (down) then the policy has caused σ to rise (fall) and thus it can be concluded that it will result in fewer (more) cartels forming in the new steady state. Intuitively, if the new policy is effective, then its adoption will immediately cause the marginally stable cartels to collapse, which, by virtue of being marginally stable, tend to be of relatively short duration. Their exit from the cartel population means they cannot be discovered. It follows that the surviving cartels are those which tend to be more stable and thus of longer duration. Since those cartels make up the pool from which cartels are discovered, the average duration of discovered cartels rises in the short run in response to a more effective competition policy.

There are at least two problematic aspects to the approach of Harrington and Chang (2009, 2015). First, the modeling of the birth process is largely devoid of economic content. The opportunity to cartelize is exogenous and unrelated to any incentives to form a cartel.[5] Second, cartel collapse occurs in the context of the Prisoners' Dilemma only because firms cannot adjust the extent to which they collude; thus, collusion is either stable or not. If the stage game was a quantity game or differentiated products price game with an infinite action space, then in response to strong demand conditions and a heightened desire to cheat, firms could reduce the extent of collusion rather than end collusion altogether. As cartel collapse is a real phenomenon, the modeling challenge is to generate a positive probability of collapse when the action space is rich.[6]

It is worth noting that Katsoulacos, Motchenkova, and Ulph (2015a) is related on some dimensions to Harrington and Chang (2009, 2015). It similarly considers a population of industries for which cartels are born and die. However, as it does not allow for stochastic market conditions, it cannot produce internal cartel collapse as an equilibrium phenomenon. However, it is richer in allowing for the probability that a cartel reforms to depend on how the cartel died; whether it died because it was caught and convicted or because a member firm cheated (with only the former occurring in equilibrium). The model also introduces another competition policy instrument: the probability that a conviction results in the cartel actually shutting down (rather than the standard assumption that it discontinues for sure). The paper distinguishes between competition policy designed to deter short-term recidivism (which pertains to the probability that a cartel continues post-conviction) and to deter long-term recidivism (which pertains to the probability that a competitive industry cartelizes). The paper provides a rich and promising framework for assessing the welfare impact of competition policy.

3.2   Cartel Participation

Though many cartels are not all-inclusive,[7] very little research has been done that examines which firms choose to participate in cartels (and how cartel and non-cartel members interact) and even less work that looks into the influence of competition policy on cartel size and participation. Here we review an approach taken in Bos and Harrington (2010, 2015).[8]

Consider an infinitely repeated capacity-constrained Bertrand price game with perfect monitoring. Firms are identical except possibly with respect to their capacities; n firms offer homogeneous products with identical constant marginal cost c. The capacity of firm j is denoted by k_j and is fixed; $K \equiv \sum_{j=1}^{n} k_j$ is industry capacity, and $K_\Gamma \equiv \sum_{j \in \Gamma} k_j$ is total capacity of cartel $\Gamma \subseteq \{1, 2, \ldots, n\}$. With market demand $D(p)$, $D(p) - (K - K_\Gamma)$ is the cartel's residual demand.

The focus is on equilibrium strategy profiles for which (1) past behavior by non-cartel members has no effect on cartel members' current behavior, (2) any deviation from the collusive price by a cartel member results in infinite reversion to a static Nash equilibrium, and (3) cartel members set a common price and allocate demand proportional to capacity. Of particular note, (1) means that cartel members do not engage in exclusionary activities against non-cartel members for selling too much. As a result, each non-cartel member's pricing behavior is its static best response, which is to undercut the collusive price and produce up to capacity. Encompassing exclusionary activities is a worthwhile research direction.

Cartel Γ faces the problem of choosing a common price to maximize each cartel member's profit while ensuring that the equilibrium condition is satisfied:

$$p^*(\Gamma) = \max_p \left(\frac{1}{1-\delta} \right) (p - c)[D(p) - (K - K_\Gamma)] \left(\frac{k_i}{K_\Gamma} \right) \qquad (3.9)$$

$$\text{subject to } \left(\frac{1}{1-\delta} \right) (p - c)[D(p) - (K - K_\Gamma)] \left(\frac{k_i}{K_\Gamma} \right) \geq (p - c)k_i. \qquad (3.10)$$

As the objective in (3.9) is proportional to a firm's capacity, all cartel members have the same preferences regarding price; and the equilibrium condition in (3.10) is the same for all firms.

The equilibrium collusive value for firm $i \in \Gamma$ is

$$k_i V^c(\Gamma) \equiv k_i \left(\frac{1}{1-\delta} \right) (p^*(\Gamma) - c) \left[D(p^*(\Gamma)) - (K - K_\Gamma) \right] \left(\frac{1}{K_\Gamma} \right).$$

In equilibrium, members of cartel Γ price at $p^*(\Gamma)$ and proportionally constrain output below capacity, while non-cartel members price just below $p^*(\Gamma)$ and produce at capacity. It is shown that if the cartel controls more capacity, then the cartel price is (weakly) higher: if $K_{\Gamma''} > K_{\Gamma'}$, then $p^*(\Gamma'') \geq p^*(\Gamma')$.

The focus is on *stable* cartels in the sense of membership or participation. A cartel is stable if (1) all cartel members prefer to be in the cartel (internal stability), and (2) all non-cartel members prefer to be outside the cartel (external stability). In characterizing the set of stable cartels, first note that cartel members always want non-cartel members to join. It is better to have a firm inside the cartel (restricting its output below its capacity) than outside the cartel (producing at capacity). Formally, if the cartel is more inclusive, then the original cartel members are better off:

If $\Gamma' \subset \Gamma''$, then $V^c(\Gamma'') > V^c(\Gamma') \Rightarrow k_i V^c(\Gamma'') > k_i V^c(\Gamma')$, $\forall i \in \Gamma'$.

In contrast, a non-cartel member may or may not want to join. Joining a cartel has the benefit that it results in a higher collusive price, because the cartel controls more capacity. However, the firm must reduce its supply, as now it is expected to produce below its capacity.

Some insight can be provided as to who is likely to be a member of a stable cartel. First, a firm with more capacity is more inclined to join the cartel, because the rise in price from joining is large relative to the proportional fall in its quantity. Second, if a firm is sufficiently small, it will not join the cartel, because the rise in price is small—as cartel capacity expands only a little—but the percentage by which it must reduce its supply is not small.

Bos and Harrington (2015) augment this structure by introducing competition law and enforcement. There is a per period probability $\sigma(\Gamma)$ that cartel Γ ends up paying a penalty. It is assumed that a cartel with more members is more likely to be discovered and convicted: if $\Gamma' \subset \Gamma''$, then $\sigma(\Gamma') < \sigma(\Gamma'')$. The penalty to firm i in the event of conviction equals $\gamma k_i V^c(\Gamma)$ and thus is assumed to be proportional to collusive value. In sum, the expected penalty of firm $i \in \Gamma$ is $\sigma(\Gamma)\gamma k_i V^c(\Gamma)$.

Competition law and enforcement is shown to undermine internal stability and can decrease the size of the largest stable cartel. By joining the cartel, a firm adds to collusive value by having the cartel control more capacity, which results in a higher collusive price. However, more members make it more likely the cartel will be caught and convicted, which raises expected penalties. Thus, the value of being in a cartel can rise when one of its members leave (especially so when the exiting firm is small). Hence, it is no longer the case that a cartel welcomes all firms. This force tends to reduce the size of the largest stable cartel. At the same time, enforcement can increase the size of the smallest stable cartel by undermining internal stability. The expected penalty reduces the collusive value, which tightens the equilibrium condition and so could cause a partial cartel to lose the ability to sustain a collusive price. Ensuring compliance with the collusive price may require making the cartel more inclusive. In sum, it appears that competition policy tends to compress cartel size, in that it makes the smallest stable cartels more inclusive and the largest stable cartels less inclusive.

3.3 Collusive Price

How does competition law and enforcement affect collusive outcomes? In practice, the collusive outcome generally means a common price and a market allocation. However, the literature has almost exclusively focused on the case of symmetric firms, so the only issue is price (with firms having equal market shares).

In thinking about the impact of competition policy on price, it is useful to consider it in the context of a broader question: What constrains the collusive price path? A cartel may not set a higher price, because a higher price is unstable; that is, the equilibrium condition is binding at the current price. Related to that factor, firms may be uncertain about how high a price is stable (e.g., there may be uncertainty regarding firms' demand functions at a higher price).[9] Alternatively, a higher price may be stable but unprofitable. Some possible reasons that it would be unprofitable are that the current price is the monopoly price (so that collusion is maximal), (industrial) buyers may resist a higher price (by postponing their purchases), and a higher price (or a bigger price change) may be more likely to lead to discovery of the cartel.

In the ensuing analysis, the focus is on how competition policy influences price when price affects the likelihood of detection (and conviction) and the magnitude of the penalty in the event of conviction. One modeling approach is to modify a static joint profit maximization model by allowing for conviction and penalties (Block, Nold, and Sidak 1981). Let $\pi(p)$ denote the representative firm's profit when all firms charge a common price p, $\sigma(p)$ the probability of discovery and conviction, and $F(p)$ the per firm penalty if convicted. Assume $\sigma(p)$ and $F(p)$ are both differentiable and increasing in price, so that a higher price makes discovery more likely and results in a higher penalty (as would be the case with customer damages and some government penalty formulas).

The cartel chooses price to maximize profit minus the expected penalty:

$$\max_{p} \pi(p) - \sigma(p)F(p).$$

Define p^m as the cartel's price in the absence of competition policy, which, under the usual concavity assumptions, is defined by $\pi'(p^m) = 0$. If $\sigma'(p^m) > 0$ and $F'(p^m) \geq 0$, then the first-order condition implies that competition policy induces the cartel to set a lower price:

$$\pi'(p^*) - \sigma'(p^*)F - \sigma(p^*)F'(p^*) = 0 \Rightarrow p^* < p^m.$$

By marginally lowering the cartel price below p^m, there is no first-order effect on profit, because $\pi'(p^m) = 0$, but there is a first-order reduction in the expected penalty, because $\sigma'(p^m)$ $F(p^m) - \sigma(p^m)F'(p^m) > 0$.

Much of the literature instead uses a dynamic approach to characterize collusive prices in the presence of competition law and enforcement. One class of dynamic models augments a standard infinitely repeated oligopoly game by assuming that there is some probability of conviction and some penalty, both of which are either fixed or depend only on the current price. Section 3.3.1 discusses models for which the probability of paying penalties and the penalty are fixed. A second class of models has the probability of paying penalties and the penalty size depend on current and past prices. By allowing for dependence on past prices, the game is no longer repeated as there are state variables. That approach is reviewed in sections 3.3.2 and 3.3.3.

3.3.1 Infinitely Repeated Game

Consider an oligopoly game with n firms offering symmetrically differentiated products and assume that a firm's demand is continuously differentiable with regard to all firms' prices. Let $\pi_i(p_1, \ldots, p_n)$ be the profit function for firm i with the usual properties of quasi-concavity in own price and increasing in other firms' prices. If firms collude, then there is a per period probability of discovery and conviction σ, which brings with it a fixed per firm penalty F. In the event of conviction, suppose the cartel is permanently shut down with probability ζ and continues with probability $1 - \zeta$. However, if a firm deviates then the cartel permanently breaks down, so that a stage game Nash equilibrium ensues.[10]

In specifying the equilibrium condition, let $\pi^d(p)$ denote a firm's maximal profit (with respect to its own price) when all other firms price at p. The equilibrium condition for collusive price p is

$$\pi(p) - \sigma F + \delta\left[(1 - \sigma)V^c + \sigma\left((1 - \zeta)V^c + \zeta V^n\right)\right]$$
$$\geq \pi^d(p) - \sigma F + \delta V^n,$$

or

$$\pi(p) + \delta \left[(1 - \sigma) V^c + \sigma \left((1 - \zeta) V^c + \zeta V^n \right) \right]$$
$$\geq \pi^d(p) + \delta V^n, \tag{3.11}$$

where

$$V^c = \frac{\pi(p) - \sigma F + \delta \sigma \zeta V^n}{1 - \delta(1 - \sigma \zeta)} \tag{3.12}$$

is the collusive value, and $V^n \equiv \pi^n/(1 - \delta)$ is the noncollusive value. Suppose the cartel chooses the price that maximizes the collusive value (3.12) subject to the equilibrium condition (3.11). Given that the expected penalty is independent of price, the optimal collusive price maximizes collusive profit $\pi(p)$ subject to (3.11). If the equilibrium condition binds, then the optimal collusive price is the highest price such that (3.11) holds.

When competition policy is made more aggressive—as reflected in higher σ and/or higher F—the equilibrium condition (3.11) tightens. If σ and/or F are increased, then the RHS of (3.11) is unaffected, while the LHS is reduced:

$$\frac{\partial \text{LHS}}{\partial \sigma} = -\delta \zeta (V^c - V^n) + \delta(1 - \zeta \sigma) \frac{\partial V^c}{\partial \sigma} < 0,$$

$$\frac{\partial \text{LHS}}{\partial F} = \delta(1 - \zeta \sigma) \frac{\partial V^c}{\partial F} < 0.$$

A higher penalty F reduces the collusive value, which reduces the payoff from setting the collusive price rather than cheating. A higher probability of paying penalties σ similarly reduces the collusive value but also increases the chances of transiting to the state in which firms are competing. If (3.11) was originally binding, then it no longer holds at the higher values for the policy parameters. If $\pi^d(p) - \pi(p)$ (which is the gain in current profit from cheating) is decreasing in the collusive price (which is true under standard assumptions), then the collusive price must be reduced to resatisfy (3.11). Hence, raising the probability of paying penalties or raising the penalty forces the cartel to set a lower price to maintain the internal stability of the collusive arrangement.

In comparing the case of legal cartels (effectively, $\sigma = 0$) and illegal cartels ($\sigma > 0$), the preceding analysis shows that, given that a cartel forms, prices and therefore markups (how much price is above cost) are lower when cartels are illegal. While that then suggests that collusive markups are lower in jurisdictions for which cartels are illegal, it may also be the case that a prospective cartel that anticipates only being able to support a low markup may find it unprofitable to form, because the incremental profit may be more than offset by the expected penalties. This suggests that we should not see illegal cartels with low markups.

The previous point is made in Bos et al. (2016). To prove it, let us use the preceding model and, for purposes of parsimony, assume $\zeta = 1$, so that conviction shuts down a cartel forever. If cartels are legal (so there is no competition law), the equilibrium condition is

$$\frac{\pi(p^c)}{1-\delta} \geq \pi^d(p^c) + \frac{\delta \pi^n}{1-\delta} \Rightarrow \delta \geq \frac{\pi^d(p^c) - \pi(p^c)}{\pi^d(p^c) - \pi^n}. \tag{3.13}$$

Define $p^n \in \arg \max \pi^d(p^n)$ as a symmetric Nash equilibrium price. It can be shown that, for any $\delta \in (0, 1)$, (3.13) holds as the collusive price gets arbitrarily close to the noncollusive price, $p^c \to p^n$. Thus, a legal cartel could, in principle, have very low markups.[11] Now consider this setting for illegal cartels. The equilibrium condition is

$$\pi(p^c) - \sigma F + \delta[(1-\sigma)V^c + \sigma V^n] \geq \pi^d(p^c) - \sigma F + \delta V^n,$$

where

$$V^c = \frac{\pi(p^c) - \sigma F + \delta \sigma V^n}{1 - \delta(1-\sigma)}.$$

It is easy to show that the equilibrium condition does not hold as $p^c \to p^N$. Given that

$$\lim_{p^c \to p^N} V^c = \frac{[1 - \delta(1-\sigma)]V^n - \sigma F}{1 - \delta(1-\sigma)} < V^n,$$

it is less profitable to collude than to compete, which implies it is not stable to collude. Hence, a legal cartel could exist with low markups (but still exceed the competitive markup), but an illegal cartel cannot exist with low markups.[12] We already showed above that if a legal cartel has the maximal markup consistent with the equilibrium condition (and it is binding), then the equilibrium condition will be violated with an illegal cartel, which implies that the maximal markup is lower. Hence, markups are higher for legal cartels than for illegal cartels. In sum, competition policy is predicted to compress the distribution of collusive markups, as it reduces the frequency of low markups and high markups.[13] That prediction is supported by some empirical evidence in Bos et al. (2016).

Thus far it has been shown that competition law and enforcement has the desired impact of making collusion less likely or less extensive. It is possible, however, for it to actually make collusion easier. The preceding analysis was based on competition policy lowering the collusive payoff more than it lowered the deviation payoff, thereby tightening the equilibrium condition and requiring a reduction in the collusive price. Cyrenne (1999) shows that competition policy can lower the punishment payoff sufficiently so that the deviation payoff declines more than the collusive payoff, in which case the equilibrium condition is loosened, thereby allowing for a higher collusive price. That is, in the presence of competition law and enforcement, the payoff to cheating is sufficiently reduced so as to make collusion more stable.

In showing this finding, Cyrenne (1999) modified the imperfect monitoring setting of Porter (1983) and Green and Porter (1984). However, the intuition can be more easily conveyed in the context of a perfect monitoring setting. Let us enrich the preceding model by assuming that the probability of being discovered and convicted varies between (1) when all firms charge the collusive price (denote the probability by σ^{co}) and (2) when a firm undercuts the collusive price which causes firms to return to competitive pricing (with probability denoted by σ^{dev}). The equilibrium condition is now

$$\pi(p) - \sigma^{co}F + \delta\left[(1 - \sigma^{co})V^c + \sigma^{co}V^n\right]$$
$$\geq \pi^d(p) - \sigma^{dev}F + \delta V^n, \tag{3.14}$$

where

$$V^c = \frac{\pi(p) - \sigma^{co}F + \delta\sigma^{co}V^n}{1 - \delta(1 - \sigma^{co})}.$$

Higher σ^{co} lowers the LHS of (3.14) by lowering V^c and increasing the expected penalty $\sigma^{co}F$. Higher σ^{dev} lowers the RHS of (3.14) by increasing the expected penalty $\sigma^{dev}F$.

Suppose detection is more likely in the event of a deviation: $\sigma^{dev} > \sigma^{co}$. If σ^{dev} is sufficiently higher than σ^{co}, then the RHS can fall more than the LHS (relative to when there is no competition law and enforcement, so $\sigma^{dev} = 0 = \sigma^{co}$) and the equilibrium condition is then loosened. If we fix $\sigma^{dev} > 0$ and let $\sigma^{co} \to 0$, then the equilibrium condition becomes

$$\pi(p) + \frac{\delta\pi(p)}{1-\delta} \geq \pi^d(p) - \sigma^{dev}F + \delta V^n,$$

where the LHS is the same as for no competition law, and the RHS is lower. Thus, collusion is easier with competition law and enforcement and, as a result, the illegal cartel can sustain a higher price than the legal cartel can.

This result may be problematic in that the assumption $\sigma^{dev} > \sigma^{co}$ is motivated by the ensuing price war from a deviation being more likely to trigger detection than a high stable collusive price. While that is quite plausible (and we will later explicitly explore how price changes impact the likelihood of detection), the model ignores the fact that the cartel had to raise price from the competitive level to get to that high stable collusive price, which would also seem to heighten detection and thereby lower the collusive payoff. This criticism aside, Cyrenne (1999) is useful for being one of the first to discuss how detection is impacted by price changes (which is more plausible than it being impacted by price levels) and noting that this could impact equilibrium conditions and thereby the collusive price.

In a related vein, McCutcheon (1997) finds that harsher punishments can be more credible with competition laws. The problem with threatening to impose a really severe punishment (such as not colluding forever or pricing below cost for an extended length of time) is that cartel members would want to renegotiate in the event of a deviation to avoid this self-inflicted harm. The prospect of renegotiation constrains the set of credible punishments and thereby limits how high a collusive price can be sustained. McCutcheon (1997) shows that if competition policy makes meetings among cartel members more costly (by raising the likelihood of discovery), then this could discourage firms from renegotiating a harsh punishment and thereby make those punishments credible. However, just as with the critique of Cyrenne (1999), the impact of competition policy on the initial meetings to form a cartel are ignored, which, in practice, are critical. On the plus side, the analysis highlights the need to formally model meetings and take into account how they are constrained by competition policy.[14]

3.3.2 Dynamic Game with State Variables: Exogenous Detection Technology

The models of collusive pricing reviewed thus far have encompassed competition law and enforcement in a rather restrictive manner by assuming that expected penalties are either fixed or depend at most on the collusive price charged in the period in which a cartel is discovered. In reality, the penalty levied on a cartel is cumulative, as it depends on duration and possibly on past overcharges. That feature of actual practice will affect equilibrium conditions. As the cartel is active for a longer span of time, the penalty if caught and convicted rises, which will influence cartel stability.

A second feature of reality that has been ignored in these models is that discovery may not just depend on the current price but rather on the price history. For example, buyers may become suspicious if there has been a series of price increases. In this section, research is reviewed that allows the expected penalty—both the probability of conviction and the size of the penalty—to depend on the cartel's history. This concession to reality introduces a technical complication, because the game is no longer repeated.[15]

Consider the infinite horizon differentiated products price game described in the preceding section.[16] If the cartel is detected in period t, then each firm pays a penalty X^t and receives noncollusive profit π^n thereafter. The penalty X^t evolves over time according to $X^t = \beta X^{t-1} + \gamma x(p^t)$, where $x(p^t) > 0$ and is nondecreasing, $\gamma > 0$, and $1 - \beta \in (0, 1)$ is the depreciation rate. If the penalty is customer damages, then $x(p^t) = (p^t - p^{bf})D(p^t)$, where $D(p)$ is a firm's demand when all colluding firms charge p, and p^{bf} is the but-for price (typically, a static Nash equilibrium price). Alternatively, $x(p^t)$ could equal some constant, in which case the penalty just depends on duration. When the cartel comes to set price in period t, it will know the state variable X^{t-1}, which is the accumulated penalty for each firm.

In allowing past prices to influence the probability of detection, it is assumed only prices in the current period and previous one matter. Let $\phi(p^{t-1}, p^t)$ denote the probability of discovery (and conviction) in period t, where p^t is the vector of firms' prices in period t, and p^{t-1} is the price vector for period $t - 1$. Presuming buyers expect a stable environment, assume that they are more likely to become suspicious when prices change:

$$\phi(\underline{p}', \underline{p}') \leq \phi(\underline{p}'', \underline{p}') \text{ and } \phi(\underline{p}', \underline{p}') \leq \phi(\underline{p}', \underline{p}''), \text{ for all } \underline{p}', \underline{p}'';$$

and when price increases are larger:

if $\underline{p}'' \geq \underline{p}' \geq \underline{p}^0$ (component wise), then $\phi(\underline{p}'', \underline{p}^0) \geq \phi(\underline{p}', \underline{p}^0)$.

These assumptions are rather mild. However, for some of the ensuing results, a stronger assumption is required, which is that there is a continuously differentiable function $\hat{\phi}$ and a summary statistic g for a price vector such that

$$\phi(\underline{p}^t, \underline{p}^{t-1}) = \hat{\phi}(g(\underline{p}^t) - g(\underline{p}^{t-1})).$$

That is, the probability of detection depends on the change in the summary statistic. The following general properties are assumed. First, if all firms charge the same price, then the summary statistic is that price: $g(p, \ldots, p) = p$. Second, a higher price vector increases the summary statistic: if $\underline{p}'' \leq \underline{p}'$ (component wise), then $g(\underline{p}'') \leq g(\underline{p}')$. Average price, weighted average price, and median price all satisfy these properties. Third and finally, it is assumed that $\hat{\phi}$ is nondecreasing in the summary statistic for price increases—if $x \geq y$, then $\hat{\phi}(x) \geq \hat{\phi}(y)$—and is minimized when the summary statistic does not change, $\hat{\phi}(x) \geq \hat{\phi}(0)$, $\forall x$. A special case is when the probability of detection is minimized when average price (across firms) does not change and is higher for bigger increases in average price. With these assumptions, detection depends only on price changes and not on the price level.

Along the equilibrium path, the state variables are the accumulated penalty X^{t-1} and the cartel's price in the previous period p^{t-1}.[17] The setting is one of perfect monitoring, for which if any firm deviates from the collusive price path, then the continuation equilibrium is a Markov perfect equilibrium (hereafter MPE). Given the dynamics associated with detection, even if a firm cheats, the resulting pricing problem is dynamic because the ensuing price path affects the likelihood of detection. While details are in Harrington (2004a), for my purposes here, just let V^{mpe} denote a firm's MPE payoff.

The cartel's problem can be cast as the following constrained dynamic programming problem where, subject to using an MPE punishment, firms achieve the best symmetric subgame perfect equilibrium in terms of expected payoff. Letting $V^c(p^{t-1}, X^{t-1})$

denote a firm's (equilibrium) value function when firms are colluding, it is recursively defined by

$$V^c(p^{t-1}, X^{t-1}) = \max_p \pi(p) + \delta\phi(p, p^{t-1})$$

$$\times \left[(\pi^n/[1-\delta]) - \beta X^{t-1} - \gamma x(p) \right]$$

$$+ \delta[1 - \phi(p, p^{t-1})]V^c(p, \beta X^{t-1} + \gamma x(p)),$$

(3.15)

subject to $\pi(p) + \delta\phi(p, p^{t-1})[(\pi^n/[1-\delta]) - \beta X^{t-1} - \gamma x(p)]$

$$+ \delta[1 - \phi(p, p^{t-1})]V^c(p, \beta X^{t-1} + \gamma x(p))$$

$$\geq \max_{p_i} \pi(p|p_i) + \delta\phi(p|p_i, p^{t-1})[(\pi^n/[1-\delta]) - \beta X^{t-1}]$$

$$+ \delta[1 - \phi(p|p_i, p^{t-1})]V^{mpe}(p|p_i, \beta X^{t-1}).$$

(3.16)

The cartel chooses price while taking into account its impact on
current profit $\pi(p)$, on the probability of detection and conviction
$\phi(p, p^{t-1})$, on the penalty $\beta X^{t-1} + \gamma x(p)$, and on the future value
$V^c(p, \beta X^{t-1} + \gamma x(p))$ through its effect on the state variables. It
does so while recognizing that the price must be incentive compatible, which requires that the payoff from setting the collusive price
is at least as great as that from deviating, as specified in (3.16). In
specifying the deviation payoff in (3.16), firm i takes into account
its impact on current profit $\pi(p|p_i)$ (where $p|p_i$ denotes the vector
in which all firms but i charge p and firm i charges p_i) and on the
probability of being caught and convicted, $\phi(p|p_i, p^{t-1})$. The latter
event results in a payoff of $(\pi^n/[1-\delta]) - \beta X^{t-1}$ and, to maintain
a common penalty state variable, there is no penalty for the period
in which a deviation occurs. In the event that detection does not
immediately occur, the continuation payoff is $V^{mpe}(p|p_i, \beta X^{t-1})$,
which is the MPE payoff associated with those state variables.

The comparative advantage of this model is in generating predic-
tions for the entire collusive price path and not just the steady state,
which, in essence, is what standard theories provide. Nevertheless,
let us start by characterizing the steady-state collusive price (in the

event that the cartel has not been caught) when the equilibrium constraint (3.16) is not binding. Letting p^* denote the steady-state price, it is defined by

$$\pi'(p^*) - \frac{\delta\hat{\phi}(0)\gamma x'(p^*)}{1 - \delta\beta(1 - \hat{\phi}(0))} = 0. \tag{3.17}$$

In the steady state, the price change over time is zero, so the probability of detection is $\hat{\phi}(0)$. Consider the effect of a one-time marginal change in price from p^*. First, there is the marginal change in current profit of $\pi'(p^*)$. Second, there is the marginal change in the accumulated penalty of $x'(P^*)$, which produces an expected present value loss equal to $[\delta\hat{\phi}(0)/(1 - \delta\beta[1 - \hat{\phi}(0)])]\gamma x'(p^*)$ (which takes into account the likelihood of detection as well as penalty depreciation). Third, there is the change in the expected penalty associated with previously incurred penalties, which is $\hat{\phi}'(0)[\gamma x(P^*)/(1 - \beta)]$, but this equals zero, since $\hat{\phi}'(0) = 0$ (as $\hat{\phi}$ is minimized at zero and is differentiable).

As described in (3.17), the steady-state cartel price is set so as to equate the rise in profit from a higher price with the expected present value of the marginal rise in the penalty from that higher price. Note that if the penalty is insensitive to price, $x'(p) = 0$, then the second term is zero, so $\pi'(p^*) = 0$, which means that the cartel charges the unconstrained joint profit-maximizing price in the long run. For example, if the penalty only depends on duration—which is captured here with $x(p) = f$ for some $f > 0$—then competition policy may constrain collusive price in the short run (which we will see below is indeed the case), but it does not constrain collusive price in the long run. What drives this result is that the probability of detection is not sensitive to small price changes, so in the steady-state, there is no first-order effect on the expected penalty from raising price a little. Hence, the cartel will raise price as long as it is below the joint profit-maximizing price. However, it is likely to raise price only gradually, because bigger price changes result in higher chances of detection. Competition policy then slows the rate at which the collusive price converges to the monopoly price.

Let us now turn to examining price dynamics. If the equilibrium conditions in (3.16) are not binding, then it can be shown that the equilibrium price path is increasing over time. This is so for obvious reasons. The probability of detection is increasing in the price change so the cartel gradually raises price to the steady-state level and, in doing so, trades off a lower current profit for a lower chance of detection. Though a straightforward implication of the model's assumptions, it is still useful to have a theory that produces a transitional price path, because many actual cartels have such price dynamics. As the cartel continues to collude and to do so at higher prices, the accumulated penalty X^t grows, which makes the cartel more sensitive to not inducing detection. As the probability of triggering detection would be higher if price is lowered (compared to keeping price constant), this dynamic provides a reinforcing reason for price not to decline at any point on the collusive price path. That property, however, necessarily holds only when the equilibrium conditions are not binding. If they are binding, then as the penalty accumulates, they can become more stringent. The reason is that the likelihood of paying penalties is lessened by shutting the cartel down, and that enhances the incentive to deviate. In that case, the previous period's price may no longer be sustainable with a higher accumulated penalty, which forces the cartel to lower price in order to maintain cartel stability. This is true even though lowering price implies a higher chance of detection than does keeping price fixed. Thus, an illegal cartel's price path could initially rise and then decline as it makes its way to its steady-state level.

Finally, let us explore the impact of the discount factor on the collusive price path when (3.16) binds. In the standard collusive model without competition law and enforcement, the collusive price is increasing in δ when the equilibrium condition is binding, because more-patient firms have a weaker temptation to cheat; they prefer to maintain future collusive profits rather than to increase current profit by cheating. That force is operative here as well, but there is

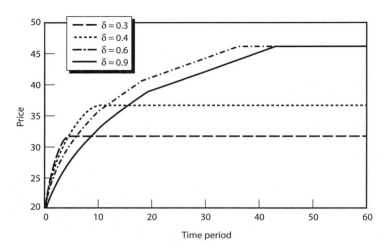

Figure 3.1
Effect of the discount factor on equilibrium price path.
Source: Harrington (2004a).

a second role for time preferences. The cartel faces an intertemporal trade-off in that a higher price in the current period raises current profit but lowers the future payoff by increasing both the likelihood of detection and the size of the penalty. As cartel members become more patient, they prefer not to raise the collusive price as fast. As depicted in figure 3.1, a higher discount factor can initially lower the collusive price path but also raise the steady-state price (for the usual reasons) which then means the price path is eventually higher.

The preceding result is shown numerically in Harrington (2004) and a related result is proven in Houba, Motchenkova, and Wen (2012) for a simpler model. They show that as δ goes to one, the optimal cartel price goes to the static Nash equilibrium price. The model is the infinitely repeated Bertrand price game, but the probability of detection is linear in contemporaneous price and the penalty is proportional to contemporaneous profit. Thus, there are no state variables. In the event of conviction, the cartel is permanently shut down with probability ζ and remains active with probability $1 - \zeta$ (in which case, it could be convicted again in the future). The best symmetric equilibrium price is characterized assuming the grim punishment. If $\zeta = 0$, then the standard result emerges, which is that the collusive price is (weakly) increasing in δ. However, if $\zeta > 0$, then the collusive price converges to the static Nash equilibrium price as δ goes to one. When δ is low, a collusive equilibrium does not exist. When δ is intermediate, there is a collusive equilibrium, and the price is set at the highest level satisfying the equilibrium condition. When δ is high, the equilibrium condition is not binding, in which case the cartel sets price at the unconstrained joint profit-maximizing price, which is *decreasing* in δ due to competition policy. As firms are more patient, they become more concerned about being detected (and permanently shut down), so they limit how high is the price, because the probability of detection is increasing in price. As $\delta \to 1$, they are content to set price arbitrarily close to the competitive price to ensure a long stream of (low) collusive profits.

3.3.3 Dynamic Game with State Variables: Endogenous Detection Technology

While these dynamic models are a useful advance, a problem is the lack of richness in modeling how the price path impacts detection. The approach is black box, in that an exogenous function is specified whereby the probability of detection depends on the price path (such as the contemporaneous price level or price change). A more foundational approach would be to model a buyer or CA as a player and characterize an equilibrium in which a buyer or CA is trying to determine whether a cartel exists and, at the same time, the cartel is trying to avoid detection. While this approach has been pursued in a static setting (which is reviewed in section 4.2), it poses a serious technical challenge in the dynamic setting.

A step in that direction was taken in Harrington and Chen (2006). Rather than model a buyer as an optimizing player, they are viewed as empiricists. A cartel is detected when a buyer becomes suspicious, which is presumed to occur when observing a price path that is unlikely to be based on the history of prices. The idea is that an anomalous price path triggers detection and what is anomalous depends on what buyers have come to expect.

Suppose that firms have a common and stochastic linear cost function $C^t(q) = c^t q$. c^t is a random walk, $c^t = c^{t-1} + \varepsilon^t$, and $\varepsilon^t \sim N(\mu_\varepsilon, \sigma_\varepsilon^2)$ and is *iid*. Absent collusion, cost shocks provide a competitive rationale for large price increases. Buyers have the null hypothesis that firms compete and will reject the null when the price series is sufficiently unlikely. The prior information of buyers is that price is a random walk $p^t = p^{t-1} + \eta^t$, where $\eta^t \sim N(?, ?)$ is normally distributed, but buyers do not know the moments of the distribution on η^t. In forming beliefs on those moments, buyers use past price changes, and it is assumed they have a finite memory of k periods, so their data set is $\{\Delta p^{t-k}, \ldots, \Delta p^{t-1}\}$, where $\Delta p^\tau \equiv p^\tau - p^{\tau-1}$. Using the sampling moments, buyers' distribution on Δp^t is $N(m_1^{t-1}, m_2^{t-1} - [\cdot])$, where

$$m_i^{t-1} \equiv \left(\frac{1}{k}\right) \sum_{\tau=t-k}^{t-1} (\eta^\tau)^i.$$

To limit the dimensionality of the state space, buyers' sampling moments are approximated by the equations of motion:

$$m_i^t = \lambda_i m_i^{t-1} + (1 - \lambda_i)(\eta^t)^i, \text{ where } \lambda_i \in (0, 1).$$

Buyers will assess the reasonableness of recent price changes by testing a sequence of the $z(<k)$ most recent price changes. Given their beliefs $N(m_1^{\tau-1}, m_2^{\tau-1} - [m_1^{\tau-1}]^2)$ on Δp^τ, the likelihood of these z price changes is specified to be a "moving" likelihood, $l^t \equiv \Pi_{\tau=t+1-z}^t f(\eta^\tau; m_1^{\tau-1}, m_2^{\tau-1} - [m_1^{\tau-1}]^2)$, where f is the normal density function. The maximum likelihood for the z most recent price changes is

$$ml^t \equiv \Pi_{\tau=t+1-z}^t \max_{y^\tau} f(y^\tau; m_1^{\tau-1}, m_2^{\tau-1} - [m_1^{\tau-1}]^2).$$

A buyer's suspicions about collusion is assumed to depend on the relative likelihood assigned to those recent price changes:

$$L^t \equiv \frac{l^t}{ml^t} = \frac{\Pi^t_{\tau=t+1-z} \, f(\eta^\tau; m_1^{\tau-1}, m_2^{\tau-1} - [m_1^{\tau-1}]^2)}{\Pi^t_{\tau=t+1-z} \, \max_{y^\tau} f(y^\tau; m_1^{\tau-1}, m_2^{\tau-1} - [m_1^{\tau-1}]^2)}.$$

The movement of L^t is approximated by the equation of motion,

$$L^t = (L^{t-1})^\xi \, \varphi(\eta^t, m_1^{t-1}, m_2^{t-1}),$$

where $\varphi(\eta^t, m_1^{t-1}, m_2^{t-1}) \equiv \dfrac{f(\eta^t; m_1^{t-1}, m_2^{t-1} - [m_1^{t-1}]^2)}{\max_y f(y; m_1^{t-1}, m_2^{t-1} - [m_1^{t-1}]^2)},$

and $\xi \in (0, 1)$.

Finally, the probability of detection $\phi(L^t)$ is assumed to be a decreasing function of L^t. In sum, the less likely buyers find recent price changes (based on the history of price changes), the more likely they are to conclude there is collusion. Such an event suggests a change in the price-generating process, and the presumption is that buyers would conclude one explanation is a change in conduct due to cartel formation.

This detection technology is embedded in an infinite-horizon oligopoly price setting, where the state variables are the lagged price, the lagged cost, the accumulated penalty, the sampling moments, and the likelihood. The cartel's dynamic problem (when equilibrium conditions are not binding) is numerically solved for the policy function that prescribes the optimal price depending on the state variables. To produce simulated price paths, the model is run for 40 periods when firms are competing, so that buyers can form prior beliefs on the competitive pricing process. A cartel is created in period 41, and it inherits the state variables coming out of the competitive phase.

Figure 3.2 shows two typical price paths and includes the noncollusive (or competitive) price path as a benchmark.[18] The collusive price path has a transition phase and then a stationary phase. During the transition phase, price steadily rises, somewhat independent

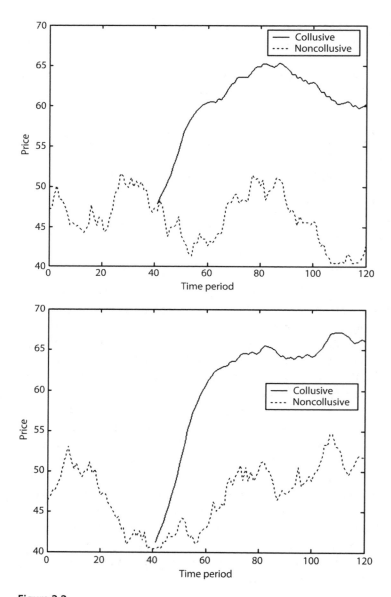

Figure 3.2
Collusive and noncollusive price paths.
Source: Author.

of cost shocks. In the stationary phase, price varies with cost but, notably, the collusive price path is less variable than the competitive price path. This is shown more systematically in Harrington and Chen (2006), where, for a large number of simulated price paths, the variance of prices over time is found to be significantly lower when firms collude. The low price variability under collusion is due to the cartel's desire to avoid triggering suspicions by making large price changes. If cost changed significantly (and cost is not observed by buyers), the cartel will want to avoid changing price too much. Even though suspicions would arise for the wrong reason—the big price change is due to cost shock and not a change in conduct—any suspicions could trigger an investigation.[19]

3.3.4 Collusive Equilibria with and without Communication

The previous models presume that any collusive equilibrium is unlawful. Thus, if firms choose to collude, they were assured of facing the prospect of penalties. However, as described in chapter 1, not all collusion is illegal. If firms decide they want to try to shift the industry from competition to collusion, there is still the decision regarding how to consummate and conduct collusion and whether to do so in an unlawful manner. Of course, it must be the case that lawful collusion is less effective than unlawful collusion; otherwise, firms would always pursue the legal variety. As only collusion involving certain forms of communication is illegal, firms can then either seek to most effectively collude by engaging in communication practices that are illegal or pursue less effective means of communication (or not communicate at all) and thereby avoid the prospect of conviction and paying penalties.

In the context of this book, the relevant question is: When does competition policy induce firms to choose collusion with less effective means of communication, and how does it change the form of collusion? To my knowledge, there are only two papers that speak to that question, though a growing (though still small) body of research characterizes collusion with communication, and some of it examines when collusion is more effective with communication. That research is likely to provide the foundation for then introducing competition policy and assessing its impact on collusion.

Firms are assumed to have private information on their costs in Athey and Bagwell (2001, 2008) and on demand in Gerlach (2009); they use costless messages (that is, "cheap talk") to possibly convey that private information and thereby coordinate on a more efficient outcome for the cartel. There is a second strand of research in which firms' sales or some other endogenous variable is private information and firms exchange messages for monitoring purposes. This line encompasses Aoyagi (2002), Harrington and Skrzypacz (2011), Spector (2015), and Awaya and Krishna (2016). Chan and Zhang (2015) model the exchange of messages when firms' costs and sales are both private information.

Our focus here is on the subset of this literature comparing collusion with and without communication in order to assess the efficacy of communication and thereby provide insight into when firms want to communicate and possibly unlawfully collude. While it seems obvious that communication will make collusion more effective, the challenge is twofold in proving it. First, communication is useful only if the messages are truthful and that requires creating the right set of incentives for firms to accurately communicate. Second, many clever and complicated ways can be used to structure equilibria without communication, which makes it difficult to characterize the maximal equilibrium payoff and thereby determine whether equilibria with communication can result in higher payoffs.

Athey and Bagwell (2001) consider a standard infinitely repeated game with perfect monitoring when firms' costs are *iid* and are private information. They compare collusive equilibria with and without cheap talk messages, where the intent of these messages is to share information about cost in order to enhance industry profit. A first-best solution requires the firms with the lowest cost in that period to supply the market, but achieving that outcome requires sharing private information about their costs, and each firm has an incentive to report that its cost is low in order to be able to supply.

It is shown that firms can be induced to provide truthful messages by trading market shares over time. Though a firm is less likely to be allocated any market share if it announces it has high cost, it is compensated with a higher market share in the future, which is more valuable in expectation, as it may have low cost at that time.[20]

Awaya and Krishna (2016) and Spector (2015) examine an imperfect monitoring setting in which firms' prices and sales are private information and firms' realized sales are stochastic. The objective is to understand when sharing information about sales is valuable in the sense that there is an equilibrium when messages are used that yields a higher payoff than the highest equilibrium payoff when messages are not used. The compliance challenge is that a firm may undercut the collusive price, realize large sales, and (inaccurately) report that its sales are not large.

In the case of Awaya and Krishna (2016), if cheap talk messages are not used, then the environment is one of private monitoring; that is, each firm must decide whether to continue to charge the collusive price based only on what it knows about its own sales. When firms are sufficiently patient and monitoring is sufficiently noisy, there exists an equilibrium with cheap talk messages that is strictly more profitable than any equilibrium in which firms do not communicate. The equilibrium with communication has firms self-report sales and impose a punishment if those reports are not sufficiently similar. To deliver that result, a necessary condition on firms' demand functions is that firms' sales are highly correlated but only when their prices are similar. Hence, if all firms set the common collusive price, then their sales will be highly similar. In that situation, the submission of an inaccurate sales report is easily detected, because firms' sales reports will fail to be nearly identical. However, when a firm deviates from the common collusive price, firms' sales are not strongly correlated (by assumption), which implies that the deviator's sales are not very informative of other firms' sales. This means it is unlikely to submit a report that is similar to those of the other firms and, therefore, a punishment is likely. In sum, firms find it optimal to price at the collusive level and truthfully report their sales which means monitoring is more effective when firms communicate their sales to one another.

Spector (2015) considers a similar situation but where each firm privately learns its sales at a high frequency (e.g., monthly) and all firms' sales are publicly revealed at a low frequency (e.g., annually). Thus, perfect monitoring occurs on a low-frequency basis, and the issue is whether firms can do better by providing reports of their sales as soon as they learn them and conditioning their prices on those reports. Keep in mind that the self-reports have to be incentive compatible, while the public reports are assumed to be factually correct. Sufficient conditions are provided for an equilibrium to exist in which firms more effectively collude by self-reporting their high-frequency sales information. The tension here is that if firms use the public reports of sales, inefficiencies are reduced because of less noise, but then punishment is delayed. However, if firms truthfully share those private signals through cheap talk messages, then they can have precise public signals at high frequency. Furthermore, it is incentive compatible to report accurately, because a misleading sales report will later be revealed by the public signal and, at that time, would be harshly punished. In equilibrium, that punishment is not used, so the threat is costless. In sum, both Awaya and Krishna (2016) and Spector (2015) show that firms reporting their sales to one another yields higher profit, which suggests a set of circumstances in which firms may prefer to collude unlawfully.[21]

There is a distinction between communication that serves to move firms from a noncollusive to a collusive equilibrium and communication that is part of a collusive equilibrium and acts to make collusion more effective through information sharing. Generally, the law is concerned with the former variety, but the latter is often part of evidence in proving liability. The research described thus far involves communication that is part of an equilibrium for the purpose of delivering more effective monitoring.

Encompassing communication for the purposes of coordinating on collusive strategies motivates the analysis in Harrington (2017). Though not part of the model, the presumption is that firms have constrained their ex ante communication to avoid acting illegally, and the implication is that they lack common beliefs about their collusive strategies. The focus is on a price leadership scheme, whereby it is common knowledge that price increases will be matched (and failure to do so results in competitive prices) but there is a lack of mutual beliefs regarding who will lead on price, at what level, and at what time. Thus, there is partial mutual understanding with regard to collusive strategies. Sequential rationality is assumed to be common knowledge. Two questions are addressed: (1) Are these mutual beliefs sufficient to result in supracompetitive prices? and (2) If they can achieve supracompetitive prices, are those prices less than what would be achieved if there were a mutual understanding of the strategy profile (as presumed by equilibrium)?

In answer to the second question, it is shown that there is an upper bound on price that is strictly less than the maximal equilibrium price (using the same punishment). Without mutual beliefs regarding the collusive price, coordinating on a higher collusive price requires some firm to take the lead in raising price. What is constraining how high price can go is the trade-off a firm faces when it acts as a price leader: It forgoes current demand and profit in exchange for higher future profit when rival firms raise their prices to match its price increase. This constraint on price is to be contrasted with equilibrium, where what limits the price is the condition that a firm finds it unprofitable to undercut it. Partial mutual understanding makes the coordination on price the constraining factor, not the stability of the price that is eventually agreed on. With regard to the first question, if firms engage in Bayesian learning regarding other firms' strategies and their prior beliefs have full support, then supracompetitive prices will eventually occur for sure.[22]

The research described thus far does not encompass competition law and enforcement. That is done in Mouraviev (2013) while taking a black box approach to communication. The imperfect monitoring structure of Green and Porter (1984) is modified to allow firms, in each period, to meet to exchange verifiable information as to their realized quantities. If firms unanimously decide to meet, then for that period, an imperfect monitoring setting is converted into a perfect monitoring setting. The cost of doing so is that collusion is now presumed to be unlawful, given that firms met and exchanged their sales information. The cartel then faces a trade-off when it comes to structuring the collusive equilibrium, because having meetings enhances monitoring, which serves to make deviations less profitable but also reduces the collusive value (because of the expected penalty).

Each period has three stages. In stage 1, after observing the previous period's price, firms simultaneously decide whether to meet and exchange (in a verifiable way) the previous period's quantities. If all firms agree, then they meet and there is perfect information disclosure. In stage 2, firms choose quantities, and a common price is publicly observed, which depends on the sum of all firms' quantities (as the product is presumed homogeneous) and a demand shock. At this stage, the current period's quantities are private information. The inference problem is that a low realized price could be due to a low demand shock or because some firm did not comply with the collusive outcome and overproduced. In stage 3, if firms met in stage 1, then the industry is investigated with probability σ, in which case a fixed penalty of F is levied.

The optimal perfect public equilibrium involves specifying a trigger price $\bar{p}$ (which lies in the equilibrium support of price when all firms produce the collusive quantity) such that if the realized price (1) is above $\bar{p}$ (and below the upper bound of the equilibrium support), then there is no meeting and firms produce the collusive quantity; (2) is below $\bar{p}$ and above the lower bound of the equilibrium support, then there is a meeting, and firms produce the collusive quantity if it was revealed that no firm deviated and punish otherwise; and (3) falls outside the equilibrium support, in which case there is punishment. Comparing this equilibrium to when firms do not have the option to exchange verifiable information on their sales, price wars (in the sense of Green and Porter 1984) do not occur and are replaced with "meetings" in equilibrium. Thus, the predicted price series is very different. It is also shown that, when the expected penalty is sufficiently low, the best equilibrium with meetings yields a higher value than the best equilibrium without meetings.

Mouraviev (2013) generates the finding that price wars are more common when cartels are illegal. If there is no competition policy, then in the context of the model, colluding firms will always meet to exchange sales information and avoid price wars. If there is a CA with sufficiently severe penalties at its disposal, then the preferable equilibrium for the cartel may be the one without meetings, which then implies the usual price wars of Green and Porter (1984).

A related approach is taken in Garrod and Olczak (2016a) though in a different informational setting with a distinct set of findings. The oligopoly structure is a capacity-constrained price game with homogeneous goods, and firms are allowed to have different capacities. Market demand is perfectly inelastic at m units, where m is stochastic, *iid*, and not observed by firms. A firm's price (and its realized quantity) are private information. Without communication, there are no public signals, so this is a private monitoring setting.[23] There is an inference problem when it comes to sustaining collusion, because low sales for a firm could be due to a rival firm's deviation or low market demand. The optimal perfect public equilibrium has periodic reversion to the static Nash equilibrium when a firm's quantity falls below some threshold. (By clever construction of the model, it is common knowledge among firms when to punish, even though there is no public signal.) A crucial feature of this equilibrium is that, when the smallest firm is smaller (in terms of capacity), then the frequency of punishment becomes greater, because it is more difficult to detect a deviation. A firm that deviates from the collusive price has demand exceeding its capacity and, assuming that a firm supplies enough to meet all its demand, its output equals its capacity. Hence, the smaller a firm is, the smaller will be the reduction in other firms' demands as a result of that deviation which, roughly speaking, makes monitoring more challenging, and that manifests itself in more frequent punishments.

The next step is to characterize equilibrium with communication. After prices are set and quantities and profits are privately observed, each firm decides whether to provide verifiable information to the other firms regarding the price it charged that period.[24] Equilibrium has firms charging a collusive price and then sharing information on their prices. A punishment ensues if the reported price is not the collusive price or a firm fails to report price. In equilibrium, there is no punishment (which is in contrast to when firms do not communicate). However, communication among firms results in a probability each period that the cartel is detected and penalized, where a firm's penalty is proportional to its capacity. Note that firms did not choose to communicate every period in Mouraviev (2013), while here communication takes place every period.

One of the central objectives is to determine when firms find it more profitable to collude unlawfully by communicating. Unlawful collusion avoids ever having to punish but comes with an expected penalty. If the number of symmetric firms decreases, then, holding industry capacity fixed, the smallest firm becomes larger. This makes collusion without communication more profitable, because punishments are triggered less frequently. Hence, unlawful collusion is less likely when there are fewer firms, because firms choose to collude without sharing information about prices. One interpretation of this finding is that tacit collusion substitutes for explicit collusion when there are fewer firms.

3.4   Summary of Findings

In summing up some of the findings, it is useful to think about them in the context of addressing two sets of questions. First, to what extent does the presence of competition law and enforcement change our understanding of collusion? How does the constraint imposed by the prospect of conviction and penalties affect collusive behavior? Are unlawful cartels predicted to operate differently from lawful cartels? Second, what is the impact of competition law and enforcement and, in particular, does it have the desired effect of lowering the collusive price, shortening cartel duration, and reducing the extent of cartel formation? Under what conditions is competition law and enforcement ineffective or even counterproductive?

In these models, competition policy is represented by the probability of conviction and the magnitude of the penalties inflicted on those convicted. Its impact on the presence of collusion can be direct when it involves discovering, prosecuting, and convicting a cartel, which then causes collusion to terminate either temporarily or indefinitely. These theories also flesh out the indirect effect of competition policy. The prospect of premature termination of collusion and the paying of penalties lowers the collusive payoff, which then impacts the equilibrium conditions. This effect could be so large that collusion is no longer an equilibrium, and therefore, cartels are deterred. But even if a cartel is not deterred, competition policy's influence on the equilibrium conditions can make cartels less stable in the sense that there is a wider set of market conditions in which equilibrium conditions are not satisfied, so that the cartel collapses. This enhanced instability translates into shorter cartel duration. A lower collusive payoff—due to shorter duration (because of shutdown by the CA or internal collapse) and higher expected penalties—may tighten the equilibrium conditions which then requires firms to set a lower collusive price if compliance is to be ensured.

Katsoulacos, Motchenkova, and Ulph (2015a) classify these three effects of competition policy as the *direct effect* from shutting down active cartels, the *indirect-deterrence effect* of deterring cartels from forming, and the *indirect-price effect* of constraining the price charged by the cartel that still forms and remains active. The theories discussed above also point out that competition policy affects the payoff to deviating, and it is possible that a more aggressive competition policy could lower the deviation payoff more than the collusive payoff (in which case the equilibrium conditions are loosened, which makes collusion easier). One must then be careful in assessing how competition law and enforcement affects the environment for collusion.

With regard to cartel birth, death, and duration, theories have generally shown that a higher rate of discovery and conviction and higher penalties have the desired effect of cartels forming in fewer markets and with shorter duration, which translates into a prediction of a smaller fraction of markets that are cartelized. Regarding cartel membership, the presence of competition policy alters the "all are welcome" policy of legal cartels. In the absence of competition policy, a cartel would always prefer a firm to be in the cartel rather than outside it, where it would undercut the collusive price and not constrain its output. However, concerns over detection can result in a cartel limiting its membership. Competition policy is then reducing the size of the largest stable cartel, which has the beneficial impact of reducing the collusive price. At the same time, the tightening of the equilibrium condition because of competition policy may increase the size of the smallest stable cartel.

The theory of collusion under competition law and enforcement has resulted in a rich set of new findings when it comes to pricing. Less dispersion of collusive markups is predicted when the cartel is illegal than when it is legal, because competition policy deters cartels with low markups from forming and constrains the markups of those that do form. Though competition policy often limits the collusive price, if the equilibrium conditions are not binding and the penalty is not sensitive to the price charged, then the steady-state collusive price is unaffected by the presence of a CA. Furthermore, if the equilibrium condition binds, it is even possible for the collusive price to be higher under competition policy, because it serves to lower the deviation payoff more than it lowers the collusive payoff. However, those conditions seem rather special.

Where the theories have yielded richer findings is in characterizing price dynamics. With standard theories of collusion, a legal cartel probably has no reason not to raise price significantly upon cartel formation.[25] But if the cartel is illegal and detection is sensitive to the price path, then the cartel may choose to raise price gradually. Broadly consistent with some actual cartels, the price path has a transition phase, in which price rises in a manner largely independent of cost shocks and is followed by a stationary phase where price is less sensitive to cost shocks than under competition. It may also be the case, however, that if competition policy discourages meetings among colluding firms, this could result in price wars that would not occur if collusion was legal. A fundamental finding in the standard theory of collusion is that the equilibrium price is weakly increasing in firms' discount factors. Competition policy alters that comparative static, because a higher discount factor can result in initially lower prices though, as with lawful cartels, it raises the long-run price.

4   Optimal Competition Policy

4.1   Overview of Modeling Issues

Chapter 3 reviewed various approaches to taking account of competition policy in a model of collusion. The purpose was to provide some insight into how making collusion unlawful and imposing penalties on convicted cartels may impact cartel formation, participation in cartels, and collusive outcomes in terms of prices and duration. I now turn to the normative task of investigating the optimal design of competition policy. If the objective is to maximize social welfare, how should the law prohibiting collusion be written, and how should it be enforced?

The starting point is to define liability and evidentiary standards. What type of behavior should be unlawful, and what amount and type of evidence should be needed to conclude that firms have engaged in illegal behavior? Of course, from the firms' perspective, all that matters is how their behavior maps to the likelihood of being found guilty; how that breaks down between liability and evidentiary standards is irrelevant when deciding whether to collude and what price to set. That observation would seem to suggest that the optimal policy design problem could be framed as the optimal choice of a mapping from firm behavior to the likelihood of conviction (along with the setting of penalties). While that simplification is true in an unchanging environment, more generally, it is misguided to conflate liability and evidentiary standards. There may be many pairs of liability and evidentiary standards that produce the same mapping from firm behavior to the likelihood of conviction, but it does not follow that they would all produce the same *future* mapping from firm behavior to the likelihood of conviction, because evidentiary standards are more adaptable than the definition of liability. In the legal realm, liability is something to be considered fixed (once the judicial interpretation of the law has settled down), while evidentiary standards continuously evolve with methods for uncovering and interpreting evidence. To take account of that evolution requires distinguishing liability from evidentiary standards.

With regard to liability and evidentiary standards, relevant questions include: What forms of collusion should be illegal? Should only explicit collusion be illegal? Should coordinated price increases be illegal even when firms do not engage in express communication? Should economic evidence (that is, based on market data) be sufficient, or must there be evidence of communication? While the literature offers some general discussions regarding the proper design of liability and evidentiary standards, to my knowledge there is no formal analysis that seeks to determine the socially optimal definitions of liability and evidentiary standards. For that reason, we will leave this important issue and move on to those topics for which there is a body of work.[1]

Given a law, its enforcement involves three stages: *detection* of firms suspected of unlawful collusion, *prosecution* of firms (and employees) suspected of unlawful collusion, and *penalization* of firms (and employees) convicted of unlawful collusion. When should firms be investigated for suspected unlawful collusion? When should firms be prosecuted for suspected unlawful collusion? When an industry is convicted of unlawful collusion, how severe should the penalty be (recognizing that the law leaves room for discretion)? A second set of issues relates to enforcement: the proper allocation of resources with respect to detection, prosecution, penalization. How many resources should be expended? How should resources be allocated across these three stages? How should these tasks be allocated between a CA and customers? A related question of importance is, how, in practice, do CAs and customers detect, prosecute, and penalize, and to what extent does it coincide with what is socially optimal? A third issue is the optimal design of penalties. What should be the statutory maximum penalty? What factors should be relevant in determining the penalty? Should penalties be reduced for cooperating with the CA? If so, should any restrictions be placed on who can receive leniency for cooperating?

In this chapter, some of the theoretical research that speaks to the optimal design of competition law and enforcement is reviewed. The literature is rather spotty in its treatment of these various issues, with a sizable body of work on the design of penalties but very little that speaks to enforcement as it pertains to detection and prosecution and, as mentioned earlier, none that addresses liability and evidentiary standards. Section 4.2 discusses some research on optimal government policy with regard to the decision to investigate and penalize and how it should depend on price and quantity. Admittedly, its focus on economic evidence (as opposed to noneconomic evidence, such as documented communication among firms) is out of sync with the usual preliminary evidence that prompts litigation and the required evidence for surviving summary judgment by a court (much less obtaining a conviction). I review it nevertheless, because it asks the right questions and is economically sound, which makes it a good model for future research that takes better account of the constraints imposed by the legal system. The remaining sections pertain to a variety of issues concerning penalties. Section 4.3 examines the optimal design of penalties, some issues related to customer damages are discussed in section 4.4, and a selective review of the immense (and still growing) theoretical literature on leniency programs is provided in section 4.5.

4.2 Optimal Enforcement

When is it socially optimal to prosecute firms for suspected collusion? In the event of prosecution and conviction, what is the socially optimal penalty? The modeling challenge to addressing these questions is embedding firms' decisions to collude and what prices to set in the context of a CA's problem of optimal policy design. As described in chapter 3, models of collusion under the constraint of competition law can be complex. Endogenizing that policy, while taking into account how cartels respond to it, poses serious technical challenges when done in a dynamic framework. The research I review uses a static model of collusion and thus ignores many of the equilibrium constraints on collusive behavior that were the center of attention earlier in the book.

The central paper here is Besanko and Spulber (1989), which I review in some detail. As an overview, a CA is assumed to monitor price and quantity and to prosecute depending on the observed price and quantity. If a conviction is achieved, then the penalty is based on the price and quantity. The CA publicly commits to a policy regarding when to investigate and how much to penalize. Having learned this policy, firms decide whether to cartelize and, in that event, what price to set. Prosecution is costly to the CA; it may be unclear whether there is a cartel, because the CA does not know industry cost, which means a high observed price could be due to either collusion or firms having high cost and competing. The research objective is to determine how to make prosecution and penalties depend on observed price and quantity in a way that maximizes expected social welfare. Given that prosecution is costly, a CA wants to be judicious when deciding which cases to pursue. At the same time, an aggressive policy could deter some cartels from forming and also influence the collusive price of those cartels that do form.

A policy for the CA takes the form $(\sigma(q), F(q))$ where $\sigma : \Re_+ \to [0, 1]$ is the probability of pursuing a case given an observed industry supply q. The social cost of pursuing a case is K. In the event of a conviction, $F : \Re_+ \to [0, A]$ is the penalty, which depends on q, and A is the maximum fine. If a case is pursued, then firms are convicted if they did collude, and they are found innocent if they did not collude. After choosing and committing to a policy, it is observed by firms. Firms have a common cost, which can take two possible values, $\{c_1, c_2\}$, and is private information to them. Given the cost realization and the announced policy $(\sigma(\cdot), F(\cdot))$, firms decide whether to cartelize. If they chose not to form a cartel, then they produce the competitive quantity. Given inverse market demand function $P(q)$, the resulting quantity under competition is q_i^o, where $P(q_i^o) = c_i$. Note that $c_2 > c_1$ implies $q_2^o < q_1^o$. If firms collude, then they choose industry supply q to maximize expected joint profits while taking into account any expected penalties. Given that competitive profit is zero, firms collude as long as expected profits net of expected penalties is positive.

The CA chooses a policy $(\sigma(\cdot), F(\cdot))$ to maximize expected social welfare subject to the constraints that firms optimally collude and, when they collude, optimally choose quantity. For the purpose of writing down the CA's design problem, let $I_i = 1$ when firms collude and marginal cost is c_i. Hence, if $I_i = 0$, then total supply is q_i^o; and if $I_i = 1$, then firms collude and q_i denotes the supply in that case. The CA's problem is

$$\max_{\sigma(\cdot), F(\cdot), q_1, q_2, I_1, I_2} \sum_{i=1}^{2} \Pr(c_i)\{I_i[V(q_i) - c_i q_i - \sigma(q_i)K]$$

$$+ (1 - I_i)[V(q_i^o) - c_i q_i^o - \sigma(q_i^o)K]\} \tag{4.1}$$

subject to $(q_i, I_i) \in \arg \max_{q_i \geq 0, I \in \{0,1\}} I[\pi(q_i, c_i)$

$$-\sigma(q)F(q)], \; i = 1, 2 \tag{4.2}$$

$\sigma(q) \in [0, 1], F(q) \in [0, A]$

$\Pr(c_i)$ is the probability that cost is c_i. Consumer value is $V(q)$, so $V(q) - c_i q$ is social welfare before netting out enforcement costs. Industry profit is $\pi(q, c_i) = (P(q) - c_i)q$. If firms do not collude ($I_i = 0$) when cost is c_i, then social welfare is $V(q_i^o) - c_i q_i^o - \sigma(q_i^o)K$, as competitive supply is q_i^o and the expected enforcement cost is $\sigma(q_i^o)K$. If firms collude ($I_i = 1$), then social welfare is $V(q_i) - c_i q_i - \sigma(q_i)K$. As is standard with the mechanism design approach, the problem is cast as the CA choosing its policy *and* firms' choice variables regarding whether to collude and the collusive quantity, (q_1, q_2, I_1, I_2), but requiring that those decisions are optimal for firms, which is captured in the constraints (4.2). Note that the penalty $F(q)$ does not enter the CA's payoff, because it is just a transfer.

One immediate property of an optimal policy is that the penalty is set at the maximum level: $F(q) = A$. Given that firm behavior is driven only by the expected penalty and that a higher probability of prosecution $\sigma(q)$ is costly in terms of expected enforcement cost $\sigma(q)K$, a CA prefers to raise the expected penalty by increasing the penalty rather than by increasing the probability of conviction. Hence, the penalty is set at its maximum.

Before further describing the optimal policy, it is useful to present the optimal policy when the CA has full information (which, in the context of this model, means that the CA knows industry cost). Policy can then condition on cost as well as quantity. If cost is c_i, then the optimal policy has $\sigma(q) = 0$ if $q \geq q_i^o$ (so there is no prosecution if supply is at least the competitive level) and $\sigma(q) \geq \pi(q_i, c_i)/A$ if $q < q_i^o$, along with $F(q) = A$ (so the expected penalty makes collusion unprofitable). This policy ensures that collusion is always deterred and that a case is pursued if and only if firms colluded. Enforcement costs are then zero.

For the case where the CA lacks information about industry cost, the optimal policy always induces a low-cost industry to collude; hence, collusion is not fully deterred. To show why this is the case, consider a low-cost industry and let us compare it colluding a little bit (by producing just below competitive supply, $q_1 = q_1^o - \varepsilon$) and colluding a lot (by reducing supply to q_2^o and thereby imitating a high-cost competitive industry). The latter is more detrimental from a welfare perspective, so the CA prefers to make it optimal for the cartel to collude a little bit rather than colluding a lot, which will occur if and only if

$$\pi(q_1, c_1) - \sigma(q_1)A \geq \pi(q_2^o, c_1) - \sigma(q_2^o)A.$$

The LHS is the low-cost industry's expected profit from producing q_1, and the RHS is its expected profit from producing q_2^o. Rearranging this condition, one needs the increase in the probability of prosecution from supplying q_2^o compared to supplying q_1 to be sufficiently high:

$$\sigma(q_2^o) - \sigma(q_1) \geq \frac{\pi(q_2^o, c_1) - \pi(q_1, c_1)}{A}.$$

Thus, as the CA raises $\sigma(q_1)$ to make prosecution more likely for a small amount of collusion, it must increase $\sigma(q_2^o)$ to deter a low-cost cartel from engaging in a large amount of collusion. By setting $\sigma(q) = 0$ for quantities slightly below q_1^o—and thereby not deterring low-cost cartels who collude a little—the CA can reduce $\sigma(q_2^o)$, which saves on expected enforcement costs.

That argument ensures that the low-cost industry is deterred from engaging in a large amount of collusion, but it results in them engaging in a small amount of collusion. The reason that is acceptable to a welfare-maximizing CA is that if the low-cost cartel's quantity is slightly below the competitive quantity q_1^o, there is no first-order effect on welfare, but there is a first-order saving in enforcement costs associated with deterring more egregious collusion through the imitating of a high-cost competitive industry.[2]

Consider the case where the cost of a prosecution K is relatively low and the cost differential is not too large, so that the high-cost competitive supply exceeds the low-cost monopoly supply: $q_2^o \geq q_1^m$ (where q_i^m is the monopoly quantity for an industry with cost c_i). The optimal policy has $\sigma(q) = 0$ if and only if $q \geq \tilde{q}_1$, where $q_1^o > \tilde{q}_1 > q_2^o (\geq q_1^m)$. That is, for some quantity $\tilde{q}_1$ less than the low-cost competitive supply but above the low-cost monopoly supply, the CA does not prosecute if quantity is at least $\tilde{q}_1$. The low-cost industry optimally chooses to collude and produces the minimum quantity $\tilde{q}_1$ that avoids prosecution. The high-cost industry chooses to compete and faces a positive probability of prosecution, $\sigma(q_2^o) > 0$.

Hence, the optimal policy has only competitive industries being prosecuted! The CA's policy is serving to constrain collusion when cost is low, rather than deterring those cartels from forming or prosecuting and convicting them. Of course, it could set $\sigma(q) = 0$ for all $q \geq q_2^o$ and thereby avoid prosecuting high-cost competitive industries, but then the low-cost cartel would restrict output more. It is worth noting that when enforcement cost K is close to zero, $\tilde{q}_1$ is close to q_1^o, so the low-cost cartel's quantity is close to competitive levels. Thus, the high-cost cartel does not collude, the low-cost cartel colludes at a very low level, and expected enforcements costs are close to zero (because K is close to zero). The first-best outcome is approximated when enforcement costs are arbitrarily small.

Souam (2001) extends Besanko and Spulber (1989) by assuming a continuum of possible costs and allowing the penalty to depend not just on quantity but also the actual cost (which is only learned ex post). Furthermore, two classes of penalty regimes are considered: (1) revenue based so that $F(q, c) = \gamma P(q)q$, and (2) profit based, so that $F(q, c) = \gamma [P(q) - c]q$. The analysis shows that which penalty regime is preferred depends on the model's parameters.[3] Like Besanko and Spulber (1989), Souam (2001) shows that it is best to accept some small reductions in output from collusion in exchange for avoiding large reductions.

The research reviewed thus far assumes that no error is made in the judicial process. If an industry is prosecuted and there is (not) a cartel, then there is (not) a conviction. Errors in determining guilt are allowed for in Schinkel and Tuinstra (2006). Three cost types are assumed, and an industry is restricted to choosing the competitive supply of one of those three cost types (which could be rationalized by assuming that any other quantity would result in prosecution). In the event of prosecution, determination of the true cost—and thus whether firms are actually colluding—is uncertain. Thus, one can think about firms being convicted if it is shown they did not produce the competitive quantity based on the CA's assessed cost (which may or may not be accurate). As above, a CA's policy is the probability of prosecuting an industry depending on the observed quantity. Now, however, prosecution could result in type I error (a competitive industry is found guilty of collusion) or type II error (a cartel is not found guilty). The optimal policy involves more collusion when the judicial process is more random. This is quite intuitive, because the expected penalty is less sensitive to whether a firm colludes; a larger type I error means firms are more likely to be convicted even if they compete, while a larger type II error reduces the expected penalty if they do collude.

LaCasse (1995) analyzes optimal competition policy in the context of bidding rings at auctions. Bidders decide whether to collude and then learn their private valuations for the object to be sold at auction. The government decides to prosecute based on the winning bid while not knowing bidders' valuations and whether firms coordinated their bids. Hence, a low winning bid could be because of a bidding ring or because all bidders have low valuations. Equilibrium involves mixed strategies: the bidders form a cartel with some probability, and the government prosecutes with some probability. Randomization is essential, because if the bidders were certain to cartelize, then the government would certainly prosecute, in which case collusion would be unprofitable; and if the bidders never cartelized, then the government would never prosecute—as it is costly—but then the bidders would want to cartelize and set a bid equal to competitive bids for high valuations. If the winning bid is sufficiently high—so that it is inconsistent with collusion—then there is no prosecution in equilibrium. Below some critical value, the government prosecutes with some probability that is decreasing in the winning bid.[4]

In assessing the Besanko-Spulber approach, it is well-founded in that the design of policy takes into account how firms will optimally respond regarding the formation of a cartel and the amount of supply. The results are appealing in that they flesh out the implications of several trade-offs faced by a CA. First, it may not want to deter all collusion because it'll require large enforcement costs; hence, it can be optimal to tolerate low levels of collusion. Second, when all cartels are not deterred, it is important to deter large quantity reductions. It also shows how lower enforcement costs translate into welfare gains through more aggressive policies. On the downside, the approach is unrealistic in at least two substantive ways. First, it presumes a CA knows the entire environment except for cost and is able to costlessly monitor quantity (or price). Detection is then trivialized when, in practice, it is very challenging. The second striking departure from reality is the presumed legal regime. Within the model, the basis for an investigation (and perhaps also for conviction) is market data in terms of prices and quantities. A case initially based on such evidence would not survive a Twombly challenge and thus would not get beyond the pleading stage in the United States.[5]

4.3   Optimal Design of Penalties

The issue of the proper magnitude of corporate penalties for deterring collusion was touched on in section 3.1.1. Here, we turn to the more interesting and challenging matter of the proper design of government fines; that is, how should fines be calculated? To cast the problem, consider the simplest setting in which there is some probability σ that a cartel member is convicted and, in that event, the penalty is equal to $\gamma B(p,q)$, where $B(p,q)$ is the base, and $\gamma > 0$ is the penalty multiple. The base is presumed to depend on market data, including the price and quantity of a firm during the period of collusion. The problem that the literature has explored and we will discuss here is the socially optimal choice of $B(p,q)$.

In practice, many factors go into the determination of the fine levied by a government. By way of example, the European Commission sets a cartel member's fine equal to $(aT + b)B(p,q)$, where $B(p,q)$ is a firm's sales in the last full business year of the firm's participation in the cartel, T is the number of years of a firm's participation, $a \in [0, 0.3]$ depends on the gravity of the offense, and $b \in [0.15, 0.25]$. A host of factors can determine an offense's gravity, which are often referred to as mitigating factors (which cause a to be lower) and aggravating factors (which cause a to be higher). Mitigating factors generally encompass those that reduce the damage from the cartel (such as terminating collusion immediately on initiation of an investigation) and assisting in achieving convictions (such as cooperating with the CA). Aggravating factors include, for example, being the instigator or leader of the cartel and being a repeat offender. While the ensuing analysis will take the penalty multiple applied to the base as fixed, in practice it depends on cartel behavior.

The analysis covers various ways of defining the base, including using revenue (as in the case of the European Commission), the overcharge, and the profit gain from collusion.[6] The research task is to compare the performance of these different approaches, where the objective is to minimize the welfare losses from collusion. The particular form of this objective is to reduce the set of market conditions under which collusion is stable and to lower the collusive price when collusion is stable. More specifically, an infinitely repeated oligopoly game is modified to allow for a class of penalty schemes, and a penalty scheme is more attractive when (1) the minimum discount factor required to support any collusion is higher, and (2) the maximal collusive price consistent with equilibrium (or some class of equilibria) is lower.

One final point should be made before moving on to the analysis. A challenge in comparing different bases is that the resulting magnitude of fines can change if the penalty multiple γ is held fixed. For example, if revenue is used, then the base is $pD(p)$; while if collusive profit is used, then the base is $(p - c)D(p)$, where p is the collusive price and c is cost. If one finds that a revenue-based formula is more effective in deterring collusion, it could just be due to the (expected) magnitude—$\sigma \gamma pD(p) > \sigma \gamma (p - c)D(p)$—rather than the design. One fix is to compare performance while adjusting the value of $\sigma \gamma$, so that expected fines are the same for the two regimes.

My coverage of these matters is based on Katsoulacos, Motchenkova, and Ulph (2015b).[7] The setting is the infinitely repeated Bertrand price game, and the expected firm penalty is $\tau B(p)$, where

$B(p)$ is the base and $\tau \equiv \sigma\gamma$. As firms are presumed to produce to meet demand and the demand associated with all firms charging the collusive price p is assumed to be a deterministic function $D(p)$, we can then suppress the quantity in the base. Collusion is sustained with the grim punishment of infinite version to the static Nash equilibrium of pricing at the common cost c. In the event of conviction, it is assumed the cartel immediately reforms, though it is likely that results are robust to allowing it to reform with some probability less than one (including even zero).

With those assumptions, the collusive value associated with the collusive price p is

$$V(p, B) \equiv \frac{\pi(p) - \tau B(p)}{1 - \delta}. \tag{4.3}$$

When collusion is stable, it is assumed a cartel is formed and chooses the price that maximizes the collusive value subject to the equilibrium condition:

$$\max_{p} \frac{\pi(p) - \tau B(p)}{1 - \delta} \quad \text{s.t.} \quad \frac{\pi(p) - \tau B(p)}{1 - \delta} \geq n\pi(p). \tag{4.4}$$

Note that it is assumed that the penalty is avoided by cheating. The optimal price is denoted $p^c(B)$, and the monopoly price is denoted p^m.

Three penalty schemes are considered. One uses revenue as the base, $B(p) = pD(p)$. A second uses profit as the base, $B(p) = (p - c)D(p)$. Given that noncollusive profit is zero (as firms price at cost), then this base is also the incremental profit from collusion. A third scheme is based on the overcharge, $B(p) = (p - p^{bf})D(p^{bf})$. The overcharge refers to how much the collusive price exceeds the but-for price p^{bf}, and typically $p^{bf} = p^n$ ($= c$ for the case at hand). Thus, the overcharge-based formula measures how much more revenue a cartel member receives in addition to the amount of output it would have produced if it had not colluded. This formula differs from the typical customer damages formula, which is $B(p) = (p - p^{bf})D(p)$, and thus applies the overcharge to actual output rather than to counterfactual output. While formulas based on revenue, incremental profit, and damages have been used in practice, to my knowledge, the overcharge-based formula has not. However, as we shall see, it has the best properties.

When the penalty is proportional to the incremental profit, $B(p) = (p - c)D(p)$, the cartel's problem becomes

$$\max_p \frac{\pi(p) - \tau\pi(p)}{1 - \delta} \text{ s.t. } \frac{\pi(p) - \tau\pi(p)}{1 - \delta} \geq n\pi(p),$$

which is equivalent to

$$\max_p \pi(p) \left(\frac{1 - \tau}{1 - \delta}\right) \text{ s.t. } \frac{1 - \tau}{1 - \delta} \geq n. \tag{4.5}$$

The optimal cartel price is then the monopoly price. While tougher enforcement (as reflected in a higher value for τ) makes for fewer market conditions such that collusion is stable, a profit-based penalty does not constrain the market price. This result is robust to allowing for $p^n > c$ and to basing the penalty on the incremental profit from colluding, which would then be $B(p) = (p - c)D(p) - (p^n - c)D(p^n)$.

Turning to the revenue-based formula, the cartel's problem is

$$\max_p \frac{(p - c)D(p) - \tau p D(p)}{1 - \delta} \text{ s.t. } \frac{(p - c)D(p) - \tau p D(p)}{1 - \delta}$$
$$\geq (\min\{p, p^m\} - c)nD(\min\{p, p^m\}),$$

where, in specifying the deviation profit, it is recognized that it is optimal to set the monopoly price when the collusive price exceeds it (an issue that is relevant in this case). The cartel's problem can be rearranged to give

$$\max_p \frac{(p(1 - \tau) - c)D(p)}{1 - \delta} \text{ s.t. } \frac{(p(1 - \tau) - c)D(p)}{1 - \delta}$$
$$\geq (\min\{p, p^m\} - c)nD(\min\{p, p^m\}). \tag{4.6}$$

The penalty acts like an ad valorem tax and thus the objective is increasing in price at the monopoly price. With regard to the constraint, when evaluated at the monopoly price, the LHS is increasing in price, and the RHS remains constant, so the equilibrium condition is loosened as price rises above the monopoly price. Thus, a revenue-based penalty scheme induces the cartel to price *higher* than if there were no competition law (conditional on collusion being stable, which is now less likely to be true). A price above the monopoly level reduces profit (before netting out the expected penalty) but lowers market revenue and thus lowers the expected penalty (because demand is elastic at the monopoly price).

Next we turn to the overcharge-based penalty, $B(p) = (p - p^n) D(p^n)$ (recall that $p^n = c$, because the Bertrand price game is assumed). The cartel's problem is

$$\max_p \frac{(p - c)D(p) - \tau(p - p^n)D(p^n)}{1 - \delta}$$

$$\text{s.t.} \quad \frac{(p - c)D(p) - \tau(p - p^n)D(p^n)}{1 - \delta} \geq (p - c)nD(p).$$

Taking the derivative of the objective and evaluating it at the monopoly price, we find it equals $-\tau D(p^n)/(1 - \delta) < 0$. Thus, the cartel's unconstrained optimal price is less than the monopoly price. If the constraint is binding, price is even lower.

In terms of the impact on the collusive price, the overcharge-based formula is preferred (in terms of welfare) to the incremental profit-based formula, which is preferred to the revenue-based formula. What is interesting is that the latter two schemes are used in practice, but the first one is not. A penalty system used in practice that is closely related to the overcharge-based formula is customer damages, which (in the case of the Bertrand price game) has $B(p) = (p - p^n)D(p)$. Both formulas use the overcharge $p - p^n$, but the overcharge is applied to the actual quantity $D(p)$ for customer damages and to the but-for quantity $D(p^n)$ for the overcharge-based penalty. Focusing on the unconstrained problem, the overcharge-based formula results in lower collusive prices compared to customer damages, too. Intuitively, the cartel is less inclined to lower price for the case of customer damages, because it raises how much they sell and thus raises the penalty. There is no such quantity effect for the overcharged-based penalty, because the but-for quantity is used.

To show this result, consider the cartel's objective when faced with the overcharge-based penalty,

$$\frac{(p-c)D(p) - \tau^o(p-p^n)D(p^n)}{1-\delta},$$

and with customer damages,

$$\frac{(p-c)D(p) - \tau^d(p-p^n)D(p)}{1-\delta}.$$

For the purposes of this exercise, the degree of enforcement is allowed to differ between the two schemes as reflected in the parameters τ^o and τ^d. If the derivative with respect to price of the objective function under customer damages exceeds that under the overcharged-based penalty, then the optimal (unconstrained) price for customer damages is higher.[8] This can be shown to be the case if and only if

$$\tau^o D(p^n) - \tau^d D(p) > \tau^d(p-c)D'(p). \tag{4.7}$$

Given $D(p^n) > D(p)$, if $\tau^o = \tau^d$, then the LHS is positive, and (4.7) holds because the RHS is negative. For the same level of enforcement, the optimal cartel price is lower for the overcharge-based formula.

However, note that the base is higher for any price in the overcharge-based formula, because quantity is higher. To have a proper comparison, one approach is to adjust the degree of enforcement so that the expected penalty is the same for the two schemes:

$$\tau^d(p-c)D(p) = \tau^o(p-c)D(p^n) \Rightarrow \tau^d = \tau^o(D(p^n)/D(p)). \tag{4.8}$$

Inserting (4.8) into (4.7) for τ^d, the condition becomes $0 > (D(p^n)/D(p))(p - c)D'(p)$, which is true. Thus, the overcharge-based formula constrains price more than customer damages even after controlling for the level of the penalty.[9]

In summing up, the authors state: "Our analysis leads to the conclusion that there is absolutely no support from welfare economics for the currently widely utilized fining structures (mainly based on revenues). Penalties based on overcharges are welfare superior."[10]

4.4 Customer Damages

Historically, the dominant form of corporate penalty in the United States is customer damages. While government fines have become substantial since the 1990s, customer damages are still probably larger in magnitude for any case involving both public and private enforcement and, of course, customer damages are the only penalty when there is only private litigation. The historical pattern in the European Union is reversed: government fines have been the only source of corporate penalties, though now private enforcement with customer damages is starting to occur.

There are several questions that can be posed with regard to customer damages. First, what is the impact of customer damages on welfare? Second, how should customer damages be defined? In practice, it is the additional expenditure by consumers on the units purchased from the cartel. However, that departs from consumer harm as it ignores the forgone surplus on those units no longer purchased by consumers because of the higher price. Third, who should be allowed to collect damages? In particular, should only consumers who directly purchase from the cartel have legal standing to sue, or should all consumers who have been harmed be allowed to collect damages?

The second question was touched on in the section 4.3, while the third question has not been addressed, though, relevant to it, some research has characterized how harm is distributed and damages are allocated between direct and indirect purchasers.[11] Factors pertinent to addressing these two questions are fairness and efficiency. Fairness is about compensating consumers who have been harmed and would, for example, call for allowing indirect buyers to sue. Efficiency is about reducing the welfare losses from collusion by shutting down and deterring cartels from forming and reducing the extent of the quantity restrictions when a cartel is operating. Broadly speaking, efficiency suggests defining damages so they are more closely tied to the incremental profit from colluding and allowing only direct purchasers to collect damages in order to enhance incentives to monitor for collusion and bring a case. In the United States, efficiency is driving the policy on customer damages as reflected in allowing for treble damages (which promotes deterrence, though customers are overcompensated) and only allowing direct purchasers to sue (at least at the federal level). In contrast, the European Union's focus is on fairness, since it only allows single damages and permits indirect purchasers to collect damages to compensate for the harm incurred. A formal analysis of the proper design of customer of damages has yet to be done.

Let us focus on the first question: What is the impact of customer damages on welfare? I also cover some intriguing loopholes and by-products of customer damages pertinent to their proper design and implementation.

4.4.1   Welfare Effects of Damages with Sophisticated Customers

If customers are aware of collusion and the prospect of damages and take that into account with regard to their purchases, what are the welfare consequences of damages? For this question to be relevant, it is best to think of industrial buyers who may be cognizant of collusion and the possibility of suing for damages. Notably, the cartel is assumed to be aware that the buyers are aware there is a cartel.

The original analysis of Salant (1987) and Baker (1988) showed that customer damages are welfare neutral in the sense that consumer harm is the same whether or not the cartel is subject to customer damages. The intuition is as follows. Though the cartel raises price, consumers raise demand because of the prospect of receiving a payment in the form of damages for each unit purchased; hence, damages act like a subsidy. Recognizing that demand is then stronger, the cartel prices above the monopoly price but ends up selling the monopoly quantity because the additional demand in anticipation of damages exactly compensates for the deterrent effect of damages on the cartel's price. Consumers are left with the same welfare as when they are not allowed to sue for damages!

This welfare-neutrality result was derived under full information (in particular, customers know there is a cartel and how much damages they will receive). Besanko and Spulber (1990) reconsider the matter under incomplete information. The model is similar to that in Besanko and Spulber (1989), which was covered in section 4.2, except that an enforcement policy for the government (regarding when to investigate and the fine to levy) is replaced by customers (who decide when to sue and seek customer damages).

The setting is static, and firms decide whether to compete (which results in price equal to cost) or to collude (which means price is chosen to maximize expected joint profit). Given the firms' (common) price, customers decide how much to purchase. The equilibrium that is characterized has firms always forming a cartel, which means customers know there is a cartel. However, as in Besanko and Spulber (1989), they do not know the common marginal cost, which is private information to the firms. If they were to sue and win, the collected damages are $\gamma(p - c)q$. While they observe price p, choose quantity q, and know the damage multiple γ, customers do not know c and thus are unsure about the amount of damages to be collected. Legal costs are assumed to be zero, so consumers sue and succeed with some exogenous probability ρ.

Though the uncertainty faced by consumers is not impacting the decision to sue, it will affect how much they demand. Anticipating being able to sue, consumers will demand more, which will tend to mitigate the welfare consequences of collusion. The net surplus to a consumer from buying q units at a price p and pursuing a case that succeeds with probability ρ when the cartel's cost proves to be c is

$$V(q) - pq + \rho\gamma(p - c)q = V(q) - ([1 - \rho\gamma]p + \rho\gamma c)q.$$

The effective price faced by a consumer is then $(1 - \rho\gamma)p + \rho\gamma c$, so customer damages again act like a subsidy, which reduces price (given $p > c$). When the likelihood of conviction is higher or the damage multiple is higher, note that demand is less responsive to the cartel's price.

In this setup, the welfare-neutrality result can break down and, more specifically, total output is higher and consumers are better off when there is a policy of being able to sue and collect damages. With private information, consumers will seek to infer cost from price. Thus, a higher price by the cartel will lead to a higher inferred cost, which will reduce demand, not just because price is higher but also because expected damages are lower due to the signaling value of price. Demand is then more elastic with respect to price, which induces the cartel to set a lower price than under full information. It is shown that if $\rho\gamma$ exceeds a critical value (but $\rho\gamma$ cannot be too high if firms are to find it optimal to collude) then, for some cost realizations, the sequential equilibrium quantity exceeds the monopoly quantity; hence, social and consumer welfare are higher with damages. If $\rho\gamma$ is below a critical value—so enforcement is sufficiently weak—then damages have no impact on quantity and welfare, and we are back to welfare neutrality.

4.4.2 Prohibition of Indirect Purchaser Suits and Bias from Damage Estimation

In the United States, only direct purchasers are allowed to sue for damages.[12] For example, if there is a cartel of LCD screen manufactures, then smartphone manufacturers are entitled to damages (because they purchased directly from the cartel members), but retail stores and final consumers do not have standing to sue, as they are indirect purchasers. Even if there is full cost pass-through by the direct purchasers, only direct purchasers can collect damages.

A rationale for this policy is that it is thought to more effectively deter and disable cartels by maximally incentivizing the agents with the best information about suspected cartels.

Schinkel, Tuinstra, and Rüggeberg (2008) identify an unfortunate implication of prohibiting indirect buyers from suing: it is possible that no litigation is brought against the cartel and collusion continues unabated. Consider a cartel that sells inputs to direct buyers who then use that input to produce a final product sold to final consumers. As in the case of the LCD example, suppose that one input is needed for each unit of the final product. A cartel can avoid direct buyers bringing a suit by sharing some of the collusive rents with those buyers. As long as the present value of those shared rents exceeds what damages the direct buyers can collect at any moment in time, it will be optimal for direct buyers to be bribed and to allow the cartel to continue rather than sue for damages and terminate the cartel. Sufficient conditions are provided such that it is possible to share the rents, dissuading buyers from suing while also satisfying the usual equilibrium condition that cartel members want to comply with the collusive arrangement. In essence, the cartel and direct buyers jointly benefit by imposing harm on final consumers.

For this tactic to be practical, however, implementation is critical. If there is evidence that the direct buyers are colluding with the cartel members, then the law allows indirect buyers to sue. A simple but effective scheme is devised: the cartel raises the input price and limits the quantity supplied to the direct buyers below their individual demands. This quantity restriction serves to constrain the supply of the final product and thereby artificially raises the final product price. The cartel benefits by receiving a higher price on the input it is selling, and the direct buyers benefit because the markup on the final product is higher due to the limited input supply. Final consumers are harmed by the higher final product price. The direct buyers do not sue (because it is not optimal to do so), while indirect buyers cannot sue (because they do not have standing). If instead any buyers could sue for the harm inflicted on them, then this scheme would not work: it is not possible for the cartel to share enough rents to bribe all buyers, because the rise in cartel profit is less than the total reduction in buyers' surplus.

Another unfortunate side effect of customer damages is identified in Harrington (2004b). There is it shown that the way in which customer damages are often estimated can cause firms to independently raise price above the competitive level after the cartel's collapse, so welfare losses continue beyond the time during which firms are colluding.

The standard formula in the United States for customer damages is $(p^c - p^{bf})q^c$, where p^c and q^c are the price and quantity for the cartel, and p^{bf} is the price that would have occurred but for collusion. The values for p^c and q^c are observed, but p^{bf} must be estimated. One common estimation method is to use pre-cartel and post-cartel data. Letting $\hat{p}^{pre}$ and $\hat{p}^{post}$ denote the average pre-cartel and post-cartel price, respectively, suppose that the but-for price is determined according to the formula $p^{bf} = \alpha\hat{p}^{post} + (1 - \alpha)\hat{p}^{pre}$, where α is the weight given to post-cartel price data (which may depend on the amount of data available in the post-cartel period relative to the pre-cartel period). Given this method for estimating the counterfactual price, a cartel member will then expect to pay damages of

$$\gamma(p^c - p^{bf})q^c = \gamma(p^c - \alpha\hat{p}^{post} - (1 - \alpha)\hat{p}^{pre})D(p^c).$$

The post-cartel game has the n firms make simultaneous (and independent) price decisions. Firm i chooses its price to maximize its product market profit less damages:

$$\pi_i(p_1, \ldots, p_i, \ldots, p_n) - \gamma[p^c - \alpha\hat{p}^{post} - (1 - \alpha)\hat{p}^{pre}]D(p^c),$$

where

$$\hat{p}^{post} = (1/n)\left[p_i + (n - 1)\sum_{j \neq i} p_j\right].$$

It is then rather straightforward that the post-cartel "competitive" price will exceed the usual stage game Nash equilibrium price.

By pricing higher and raising the post-cartel price, a firm causes the estimated but-for price to be higher, which lowers damages. Welfare losses then continue into the post-cartel phase.

4.5 Leniency Programs

The Corporate Leniency Program of the U.S. Department of Justice's Antitrust Division gives a member of a cartel the opportunity to avoid government penalties if it is the first to report the cartel and fully cooperate. Since its revision in 1993, the Program has been flush with applications that have produced many cases and convictions. Shortly after the revamped leniency program started producing applications, the European Commission instituted its own program in 1996, and a decade later, 24 out of 27 European Union members had one. Globally, leniency programs are present in more than 50 countries and jurisdictions.

In light of the widespread adoption and usage of leniency programs, a vast and growing body of scholarly work examines the effect and design of these programs. Initially reviewed in Spagnolo (2008), the literature has greatly expanded since that survey. When discussing theoretical research on the topic, two classes of questions are addressed. First, what is the impact of a corporate leniency program (hereafter CLP) on cartel formation, duration, prices, probability of conviction, and expected penalties? Second, what is the optimal design of a CLP from the perspective of deterring cartels, reducing cartel duration, and lowering collusive prices? Should all penalties be waived, or should there be partial leniency? How many firms should be able to receive leniency? Should leniency be provided only before an investigation? Should ringleaders and recidivists be ineligible for leniency?[13]

A CLP can influence firms' behavior at the time of cartel formation, during the operation of a cartel, and after the death of a cartel. With regard to the post-cartel phase, how does a CLP affect the probability of conviction by possibly inducing self-reporting? For the cartel phase, a key consideration is how a CLP affects the payoff to setting the collusive price (through its effect on the collusive value) and the payoff to cheating (through its effect on the expected penalty upon cartel collapse). By influencing the equilibrium condition, it affects the prices that the cartel can sustain as well as cartel duration. Finally, a CLP's anticipated effect on the collusive price, cartel duration, and, more generally, collusive value will influence whether a cartel forms. Let us consider research in each of the three phases of a cartel: (1) prior to its formation, (2) during its lifetime, and (3) after it has collapsed.

4.5.1 Post-Cartel Phase

Let us suppose that a cartel has collapsed, in which case the only decision of the former cartelists is whether to apply for leniency. This setting is examined in Harrington (2013a) when firms have different information about the attractiveness of applying for leniency. Consider a cartel composed of two firms that independently decide whether to apply for leniency in order to minimize expected penalties. If a firm is convicted without having received leniency, it pays a fine $F > 0$; if it receives leniency, then its fine is θF, where $\theta \in [0, 1)$, so more leniency is associated with a lower value of θ. Relevant to the decision to apply for leniency is the likelihood ρ of conviction by the CA when no firm has become a leniency awardee. The likelihood ρ is a random variable from the perspective of firms and, prior to making a leniency decision, firm i receives a private signal $s_i \in [\underline{s}, \overline{s}]$ of ρ. After learning their signals, firms simultaneously decide whether or not to apply for leniency. A strategy for a firm is then of the form: $\phi : [\underline{s}, \overline{s}] \rightarrow \{\text{Apply, Do not apply}\}$. Though firm i does not get to observe firm j's signal, it will have some information, because s_i and s_j are positively correlated. Let $H(s_j|s_i)$ be firm i's cdf on firm j's signal conditional on its own signal. To capture the positive correlation between firms' signals, assume that if $s'' > s'$, then $H(\cdot|s_i = s'')$ weakly first-order stochastically dominates $H(\cdot|s_i = s')$. A higher signal for a firm results in it attaching more probability to high signals for its rival.

If only one firm applied for leniency, then it pays a penalty of θF and the other firm pays F (hence, it is assumed conviction occurs for sure because of a cooperating cartel member). If both firms applied for leniency, then each has an equal chance of being the one chosen to receive leniency, so the expected fine is $\left(\frac{1+\theta}{2}\right) F$. If no one applied, then firms are convicted with probability ρ and each pays F, which means firm i's expectation on its penalty is $E[\rho|s_i]F$, where $E[\rho|s_i]$ is its expectation on ρ conditional on its signal. It is assumed that $E[\rho|s_i]$ is increasing in s_i.

There is always an equilibrium in which both firms apply for leniency independent of their signals, because a firm lowers its expected penalty from F to $\left(\frac{1+\theta}{2}\right) F$ by applying when the other firm is expected to do so. Let us focus instead on the Pareto-efficient symmetric equilibrium. In this case, a firm applies for leniency if and only if the likelihood attached to the CA prosecuting and convicting the firm is sufficiently high, which means there is a critical threshold, denoted x, for the signal; that is, $\phi(s_i)=$ Apply, if and only if $s_i > x$.

In equilibrium, firm 1 applies for leniency if and only if

$$\underbrace{E[\rho|s_1, s_2 \le x] - \theta}_{\text{Prosecution effect}} > \underbrace{-\left(\frac{1-\theta}{2}\right)\left[\frac{1 - H(x|s_1)}{H(x|s_1)}\right]}_{\text{Preemption effect}}. \tag{4.9}$$

The LHS is referred to as the *prosecution effect*—it deals with beliefs about the CA's probability of a successful prosecution (without use of the leniency program). A firm's expectation is based on its own signal but also on its rival's signal being below the equilibrium threshold x, so that it chooses not to apply (for otherwise the value of ρ would not matter). With private signals, a firm is not certain about what the other firm will do. Even if firm 1's signal is very low—suggesting that being caught by the CA is unlikely and thus firms should not apply for leniency (that is, the prosecution effect is weak)—it realizes that firm 2's signal could be high, in which case firm 2 would apply. Examining the RHS of (4.9), note that $1 - H(x|s_1)$ is the probability that a rival applies for leniency conditional on a firm's signal. The higher it is, the more likely (4.9) is to be satisfied, which means applying for leniency is optimal. There is then a second reason for a firm to apply for leniency, quite independent of whether it thinks the CA will catch it. This *preemption effect* captures a firm's concern with its rival applying for leniency prior to the firm itself having information that the CA is a serious threat.

If the leniency program is sufficiently generous (that is, θ is sufficiently low), the unique symmetric Bayes-Nash equilibrium (when strategies are defined by a critical threshold) is for firms to apply for leniency for all signals. No matter how generous leniency is, as long as some penalties are not waived (that is, $\theta > 0$), it is possible that firm 1 could receive a sufficiently weak signal that it would prefer not to apply for leniency on the basis that the CA is unlikely to convict; that is, $E[\rho|s_1] < \theta$. Of course, firm 1 is also concerned with the prospect of firm 2 applying. Suppose, by the same argument, it takes a really weak signal for firm 2 not to apply. Even if firm 1's signal is extremely weak, firm 1 will find it very unlikely that firm 2's signal is also extremely weak. Given that firm 1 then believes that firm 2 is likely to apply, firm 1 finds it optimal to apply as well, regardless of the signal that it receives. The prosecution effect can then be very weak, but due to the strength of the preemption effect, firms apply for leniency.

Comparing this equilibrium with one for which firms' private signals are made public is useful for drawing some implications competition policy. Suppose a CA performs dawn raids on firms 1 and 2, and assume that firm i's private signal regarding the strength of the CA's case, s_i, is based on the evidence collected from firm i during that raid. Should the CA share that evidence with the firms? That is, does the CA want signals s_1 and s_2 to be public information to firms 1 and 2? The analysis suggests that the CA should not share the evidence because of the preemption effect when firms have private information. In Harrington (2012), an example is provided that illustrates this result. There it is assumed the probability of conviction equals the sum of the firms' signals, $\rho = s_1 + s_2$, where s_1 and s_2 are independent with a uniform distribution on $[0, 0.5]$. The probability of conviction with private signals is higher (lower) than that with public signals when $\theta < .715$ ($\theta > .715$). As long as the leniency program is sufficiently generous, conviction is higher by maintaining the asymmetry in beliefs.

Other research also examines strategic behavior in the post-cartel phase. Silbye (2010) assumes that ρ is common knowledge but allows each firm to possess evidence that it could submit to convict the other firm if it applied for leniency; $\varepsilon_i \in [0, 1 - \rho]$ is the evidence possessed by firm i to assist in convicting firm j and is private information to firm i. If firm i receives leniency then firm j's expected penalty is $(\rho + \varepsilon_i)F$. Also assuming that there is no private information among firms, Gärtner (2013) considers a continuous-time dynamic setting in which firms face a probability ρ^t at time t that they will be convicted, where ρ^t follows a Markov process. One can interpret ρ^t evolving as evidence regarding a case is discovered. Firms face a waiting game: Should a firm report so as to preempt other firms or wait and hope that no firm reports and the CA is unable to convict? The main result is that either all firms report immediately or not at all. Concerns about preemption prevent an equilibrium in which firms do not apply for leniency until ρ^t reaches some threshold. For if there were such an equilibrium, a firm would apply when ρ^t is just shy of that threshold, which is contrary to equilibrium. It would be extremely interesting to extend that model to allow for firms to have asymmetric information about ρ^t.

Sauvagnat (2015) introduces an innovative twist by giving private information to the CA and allowing it to strategically decide whether to open an investigation. The CA receives a private signal—good or bad. Conditional on receiving a good signal, the probability of conviction (if no firm uses the leniency program) is ρ, and conditional on receiving a bad signal, the probability of conviction is zero. After receiving this signal, the CA launches an investigation for sure when the signal is good and with probability

ω when the signal is bad. Given that an investigation is launched, firms simultaneously decide whether to apply for leniency. The CA commits to a policy (ω, θ) at the start of the game, and it is publicly observed. Given (ω, θ), firms collude if it is incentive compatible. A continuum of heterogeneous markets exists, and the CA chooses (ω, θ) to minimize the fraction of industries cartelized at any time. The critical property of equilibrium is that the optimal value of ω is the highest value such that firms are induced to apply for leniency in response to an investigation. Note that if $\omega > 0$, then the CA is launching an investigation even though it knows it will fail to deliver a conviction unless a firm applies for leniency. The purpose is to induce firms to apply for leniency out of concern that the CA may have adequate evidence to convict (that is, its signal is good). The problem with setting ω too high is that it can dissuade firms from applying, because the higher is ω, the more likely it is that the CA has weak evidence conditional on it having opened an investigation. Further research into the strategic role that the CA can play in the post-cartel phase is needed.

4.5.2 Cartel Phase

Prior to reviewing some of the research exploring the influence of a CLP on the behavior of an active cartel, it is worth noting that there is variation in the literature regarding some basic assumptions. Concerning the extensive form, some papers assume that firms choose price prior to a possible investigation, while other papers assume firms learn about a possible investigation prior to choosing price. Given that investigations are long lasting and price is often easy to change, the latter specification seems more natural, though the best extensive form is to allow price to be chosen both before and after an investigation (as in Chen and Rey 2013). In terms of a firm's calculus when it contemplates deviating from the collusive price, some papers do not allow a firm to simultaneously cheat and apply for leniency. There seems to be no reason to rule out such a possibility. Also, some papers assume that a deviating firm is not prosecuted and penalized. This assumption runs contrary to common legal practice, which attributes liability to agreeing to coordinate on price, irrespective of whether a firm follows through with that agreement.

Variation in Enforcement Harrington (2008b) explores the incentives to apply for leniency and derives the optimal amount of leniency when the likelihood of conviction varies over time. Consider an industry with n firms that engage in an infinitely repeated Prisoners' Dilemma with collusive profit π^c. Assuming that they have been colluding, the CA launches an investigation with probability $\omega \in (0, 1]$. In the event of an investigation, ρ is randomly drawn according to the cdf G and is the probability that the cartel is detected and convicted (in the absence of someone coming forward under the leniency program). ρ is realized at the beginning of a period (when there is an investigation) and is common knowledge to the firms before each decides whether to collude and whether to seek leniency. If a firm applies for the leniency program, then the cartel is detected and convicted. A firm that receives leniency pays a penalty of θF, where $\theta \in [0, 1]$. If m firms simultaneously decide to apply, then each has an expected penalty of $\left(\frac{m-1}{m}\right)F + \left(\frac{1}{m}\right)\theta F$. If no firm seeks leniency, then with probability ρ, the cartel is detected and each firms pays F and earns noncollusive profit π^n in all future periods; with probability $1 - \rho$, the cartel is not detected and the game moves forward. As long as the cartel remains intact, there is a chance of an investigation with a subsequent drawing of ρ. In contrast to Gärtner (2013), ρ is *iid* over time.

The analysis focuses on a class of subgame perfect equilibria with the following properties. First, a deviation with a low price is punished by infinite reversion to a static Nash equilibrium. Second, there is a critical threshold ρ^o such that: if $\rho \in [0, \rho^o]$, then a firm sets the collusive price and if $\rho \in (\rho^o, 1]$, then a firm sets the competitive price and, in addition, applies to the CLP when $\rho \in (\theta, 1]$. The critical threshold ρ^o for which the cartel collapses is determined as part of the equilibrium.

The binding equilibrium condition is when, in the event of an investigation, $\rho \in [0, \rho^o]$ and firms collude:

$$\pi^c + \delta(1-\rho)E[V^c|\rho^o,\theta] + \delta\rho(V^n - F)$$
$$\geq \pi^d + \delta V^n - \delta \min\{\rho,\theta\}F,$$

where π^d is the deviation profit, and $V^n \equiv \pi^n/(1-\delta)$. The expected future payoff from continued collusion is $E[V^c|\rho^o,\theta]$ and is defined recursively by

$$E[V^c|\rho^o,\theta] = (1-\omega)V^c(0,\rho^o,\theta) + \omega \int_0^1 V^c(\rho,\rho^o,\theta)dG(\rho),$$

where

$$V^c(\rho,\rho^o,\theta) = \begin{cases} \pi^c + \delta(1-\rho)E[V^c|\rho^o,\theta] \\ \quad + \delta\rho(V^n - F), & \text{if } 0 \leq \rho \leq \rho^o \\ V^n - \rho\delta F, & \text{if } \rho^o < \rho \text{ and } \rho \leq \theta \\ V^n - \left(\dfrac{n-1+\theta}{n}\right)\delta F, & \text{if } \rho^o < \rho \text{ and } \theta < \rho \end{cases}$$

When $\rho \leq \rho^o$, firms continue colluding, and if they escape conviction, then they go on to collude again tomorrow and receive a future expected payoff of $E[V^c|\rho^o,\theta]$. If $\rho > \rho^o$, then the cartel collapses, so firms earn the noncollusive payoff V^n. If the cartel collapses and $\rho \leq \theta$, then they incur an expected penalty of ρF, while if $\rho > \theta$, then they race for leniency, and the expected penalty is $\left(\frac{n-1+\theta}{n}\right)F$.

Equilibrium requires that it is optimal for firms to collude when $\rho \leq \rho^o$. If ω is sufficiently close to zero and δ is sufficiently close to one, then a collusive equilibrium exists. The focus is on the equilibrium with the highest collusive value, which is the one with the highest average cartel duration (that is, the highest equilibrium value for ρ^o, which is denoted $\bar{\rho}(\theta)$). The CA chooses a leniency policy, which is a value for $\theta \in [0,1]$, to minimize the average duration of a cartel, $\frac{1}{1-(1-\omega)G(\bar{\rho}(\theta))}$.

Let us gain some insight into how θ affects $\bar{\rho}(\theta)$ and thereby cartel stability. Consider values for θ such that $\theta < \bar{\rho}(\theta)$. A firm that considers cheating when $\rho = \bar{\rho}(\theta)$ will use the leniency program, since doing so lowers the expected fine from $\bar{\rho}(\theta)F$ to θF. Hence, lowering θ (making the program more lenient) reduces the penalty paid by a deviator and thereby increases the payoff to cheating. This effect, referred to as the Deviator Amnesty Effect, serves to make collusion more difficult. It is also true, however, that lowering θ raises the collusive payoff and thus makes collusion less difficult. Though θ does not affect the current period's collusive profit, it influences the future expected collusive payoff. Firms realize that, in some future period, ρ could exceed $\bar{\rho}(\theta)$, in which case the likelihood of detection is sufficiently high that they stop colluding and each firm applies for leniency. The expected fine at that time is then $\left(\frac{n-1+\theta}{n}\right) F$, which is increasing in θ. This effect, which is referred to as the Cartel Amnesty Effect, has the implication that a lower value for θ reduces the future expected discounted penalty from continuing to collude and thus raises the value of colluding. These effects were present in the pioneering work of Motta and Polo (2003) as well as in Ellis and Wilson (2001) and Spagnolo (2003).

As the Deviator Amnesty Effect raises the payoff to cheating and the Cartel Amnesty Effect raises the payoff to colluding, they work in opposite directions regarding the incentives to collude. However, it is not difficult to see that the Deviator Amnesty Effect is larger, so that collusion is more difficult with a lower value for θ. The reason is that the marginal effect of θ on the deviator's fine is $-F$, since it would be the only firm applying for leniency. The Cartel Amnesty Effect involves using the CLP in the future with some probability (so the marginal effect is smaller). In addition, the Cartel Amnesty Effect assumes that all cartel members apply, so at that time, the marginal effect is $-F/n$. In sum, if these were the only two effects operating, then it is clear that collusion is more difficult with a more lenient amnesty policy.

Now consider values for θ such that $\theta > \bar{\rho}(\theta)$. A marginal change in θ has no effect on the deviator's payoff, because the marginal type, $\rho = \bar{\rho}(\theta)$, would not use the leniency program as such a firm prefers to receive an expected fine of $\bar{\rho}(\theta)F$ rather than a certain fine of θF. The Deviator Amnesty Effect is then absent. The impact of changing θ on the equilibrium condition comes down to its impact on the future expected collusive payoff. If the Cartel Amnesty Effect was the only force at work, then lowering θ would raise the collusive payoff and, since it leaves the deviator's payoff unaffected, collusion is made easier. A more lenient policy would then enhance cartel stability, contrary to the intent of the program.

However, there is yet another effect that can instead cause the collusive payoff to be *increasing* in θ; it is referred to as the Race to the Courthouse Effect. Recall that the cartel stops colluding when $\rho > \bar{\rho}(\theta)$ but only uses the leniency program when $\rho > \theta (> \bar{\rho}(\theta))$. Let us consider a cartel member's expected penalty in the event that $\rho > \bar{\rho}(\theta)$:

$$\text{Expected penalty} = \begin{cases} \rho F, & \text{if } \rho \in (\bar{\rho}(\theta), \theta] \\ \left(\dfrac{n-1+\theta}{n} \right) F, & \text{if } \rho \in (\theta, 1] \end{cases}.$$

Since $\left(\frac{n-1+\theta}{n} \right) F > \theta F$, there is a discontinuity at $\rho = \theta$. As soon as ρ exceeds θ, it is optimal for a firm to apply for leniency, even if no other firm does so. This is true for all firms, so behavior switches from no firms applying for leniency when $\rho \in (\bar{\rho}(\theta), \theta]$ to all firms doing so when $\rho \in (\theta, 1]$, which results in a discontinuous increase in the expected penalty from θF to $\left(\frac{n-1+\theta}{n} \right) F$. Hence, an increase in leniency can cause firms to "race to the courthouse" to apply for leniency, which increases expected penalties and lowers the expected collusive payoff. In sum, the Cartel Amnesty Effect and the Race to the Courthouse Effect are counteracting, and it is not immediately clear what the effect of granting more leniency is.

Taking account of the Deviator Amnesty Effect, the Cartel Amnesty Effect, and the Race to the Courthouse Effect, it is shown to be optimal for the CA to provide maximal leniency, so $\theta^* = 0$, when G is weakly concave. While it is possible to construct examples whereby partial leniency is optimal, the most plausible conditions support maximal leniency.[14]

Leniency Before and After an Investigation   A focus of Chen and Rey (2013) is to consider the decision of whether to allow a firm to receive leniency only if it applies prior to the start of an investigation or whether it should receive leniency even after an investigation has started. Many programs allow for both, though some (such as the European Union's CLP) grant less leniency after an investigation, while others (such as the U.S. program) allow the same amount.

A special case of the Prisoners' Dilemma is considered: the Bertrand price game with two prices, in which case $\pi^n = 0$, and $\pi^d = n\pi^c$. If firms are colluding, then the extensive form has each firm decide whether to set the collusive price or undercut it, and also whether to apply for leniency (which would be done before an investigation). With probability ω, an investigation is begun, at which time firms again decide whether to apply for leniency (if the CLP allows leniency after the start of an investigation). Conviction occurs if one or more firms apply for leniency, and the probability of a conviction is ρ if no one applies (and there was an investigation). A firm that received leniency before (after) an investigation starts pays a fraction θ_b (θ_a) of the penalty. It is also assumed that a convicted cartel immediately reforms. Finally, it is assumed that industries vary in π^c and otherwise are identical. This heterogeneity implies that, for a given policy, collusion is stable only in some industries. The objective of the CA is to minimize the set of industries (that is, the set of values for π^c) such that collusion is stable.

The collusive payoff when firms do not apply for leniency before or after the start of an investigation is $\frac{\pi^c - \omega\rho F}{1-\delta}$. For it to be an equilibrium for firms to collude and not report, that payoff must be at least as high as the payoffs from undercutting price and one of the following conditions: (1) not applying for leniency with a payoff of $n\pi^c - \omega\rho F$, (2) applying for leniency prior to an investigation with a payoff of $n\pi^c - \theta_b F$, or (3) applying for leniency if there is an investigation, with a payoff of $n\pi^c - \omega\theta_a F$. In addition, a firm must prefer collusion and not reporting to collusion and applying for leniency when there is an investigation, which requires $-\rho F + \delta \left(\frac{\pi^c - \omega \rho F}{1 - \delta} \right) \geq -\theta_b F$. Note that leniency does not affect the collusive payoff and can only raise the deviation payoff, so a CLP is tightening the equilibrium condition and thereby making collusion more difficult; that is, collusion (with no reporting) is an equilibrium for a smaller set of values for π^c when there is a CLP.

Next consider an equilibrium in which firms collude and report prior to an investigation. The collusive payoff is

$$\frac{\pi^c - \left(\frac{n - 1 + \theta_b}{n} \right) F}{1 - \delta}.$$

The only deviation is to undercut price while still applying for leniency, for which the payoff is $n\pi^c - \left(\frac{n - 1 + \theta_b}{n} \right) F$. The equilibrium condition can be written as

$$\pi^c \geq \frac{\delta \left(\frac{n - 1 + \theta_b}{n} \right) F}{1 - n(1 - \delta)}.$$

If $\frac{n - 1 + \theta_b}{n} < \omega \rho$, so that the cartel prefers to report, then more leniency reduces the expected penalty and thereby encourages collusion.

When leniency is only offered before an investigation (so $\theta_a = 1$), it is optimal to offer some before-investigation leniency ($\theta_b < 1$)—to enhance the incentive to deviate when firms do not report in equilibrium and thereby destabilize marginal cartels—but not so much leniency that it becomes an equilibrium for the cartel to use leniency before an investigation (which would serve to stabilize more cartels). Practically, the latter effect is unlikely to be relevant, because it requires $\omega \rho > 1/2$, which seems extreme.

Now consider designing an optimal CLP when leniency can also be offered after an investigation begins. There are more deviation strategies for firms as, for example, a firm could undercut price but then apply for leniency only if an investigation is launched. But there are also more collusive strategies; for example, all firms applying for leniency in the event of an investigation. Consider a strategy in which firms collude but do not report either before or after an investigation begins. The possibility of leniency after an investigation can raise the payoff to deviating when the expected penalty from applying after an investigation is less than the expected penalty from applying before: $\omega\theta_a < \theta_b$. As the deviator's payoff is higher (while the collusive payoff is unchanged), the possibility of post-investigation leniency destabilizes a marginal cartel. But one must be careful not to make colluding and reporting (when there is an investigation) an attractive strategy. The payoff from it is less than the collusive payoff from never reporting when

$$\frac{\pi^c - \omega\rho F}{1 - \delta} \geq \frac{\pi^c - \omega\left(\frac{n-1+\theta_a}{n}\right)F}{1 - \delta} \Rightarrow \theta_a > 1 - n(1 - \rho).$$

Combining the condition that encourages a deviator to report after an investigation with the condition that discourages the cartel from reporting after an investigation, we have $\theta_b/\omega > \theta_a > 1 - n(1 - \rho)$. It is shown that if an investigation is unlikely to deliver a conviction (that is, ρ is low), offering leniency after an investigation (that is, $\theta_a < 1$) can destabilize collusion by inducing a firm to deviate and report in the event of an investigation without causing industries to collude and report in case of an investigation.

4.5.3   Pre-Cartel Phase

An issue not yet accounted for is how policies of leniency and non-leniency can affect each other. Thus far, non-leniency enforcement has been represented by the parameter σ (or $\omega\rho$), which is the probability of detection, prosecution, and conviction. As a cartel member will apply for leniency only if it believes that doing so is better than running the risk of being caught and convicted, non-leniency enforcement is integral to the efficacy of a CLP. If σ is low, then a firm will not be inclined to use the CLP; while if σ is high, then cartel members will race to apply for leniency. Furthermore, it is natural to expect that the introduction of a CLP will change the level of non-leniency enforcement. A CLP may cause a CA's scarce resources and attention to shift from non-leniency cases to leniency cases. However, that does not necessarily imply that non-leniency enforcement is weaker. If a CLP results in there being fewer cartels, then there will be fewer non-leniency cartel cases, in which case the authority may have ample resources to effectively prosecute them. Furthermore, a CA can adjust its enforcement policy in response to the number of leniency applications. Thus, while we expect non-leniency enforcement to change when a CLP is put in place, it is not clear whether enforcement will be weakened or strengthened.

Harrington and Chang (2015) develop and explore a theoretical framework to understand when CLPs are likely to be effective in reducing the number of cartels while taking into account their impact on enforcement through traditional means. The model augments the birth-and-death process developed in Harrington and Chang (2009) by introducing a CLP, endogenizing the intensity of non-leniency enforcement, and allowing a CA to decide on its caseload. The reader should review section 3.1.2 before proceeding.

In Harrington and Chang (2009), σ is an exogenous parameter that is now endogenized. First note that σ is the compound probability of three events: (1) a cartel is discovered by the CA, (2) the CA decides to prosecute, and (3) the CA is successful in its prosecution and penalties are levied. The probability of discovery $q \in (0, 1)$ is assumed to be exogenous. Of those reported cases, the CA controls the fraction to investigate, which is denoted by $r \in (0, 1]$. And, of those cases discovered and prosecuted, the CA is successful in a fraction $s \in [0, 1]$ of them. It is assumed the fraction of cases won equals $v : [0, 1] \rightarrow [0, 1]$. The fraction v is a continuous decreasing function of the CA's caseload, which depends on the mass of leniency cases L and the mass of non-leniency cases R. The caseload is $\lambda L + R$, where $\lambda \in (0, 1]$, because leniency cases may take up fewer resources than those cases lacking an informant. In sum, the probability that a cartel pays penalties is $\sigma = q \times r \times s = q \times r \times v(\lambda L + R)$. Results are robust to r (as long as $r > 0$), and one could presume that the CA chooses its caseload to minimize the cartel rate.

Three steps are used in the construction of an equilibrium. The first two steps are:[15]

• Step 1: Given σ, solve for equilibrium collusive behavior for a type-η industry, which means finding the critical threshold $\phi^*(\sigma, \eta)$ such that the cartel collapses if and only if the random market condition π exceeds $\phi^*(\sigma, \eta)$. As π has cdf H, the probability of collapse is $1 - H(\phi^*(\sigma, \eta))$.

• Step 2: Given σ and $\phi^*(\sigma, \eta)$, solve for the equilibrium cartel rate $C(\sigma, \eta)$ for the set of type-η industries. In the equilibrium that is characterized, leniency is at most used when a cartel dies, so leniency does not shut down active cartels. Given that a cartel is born with exogenous probability κ and dies when $\pi > \phi^*(\sigma, \eta)$ or when it is caught and convicted (which occurs with probability σ), a Markov process on cartel birth and death is constructed. The stationary fraction of type-η industries for that process is $C(\sigma, \eta)$. Integrating $C(\sigma, \eta)$ over type-η industries and using the cdf G on η, we can derive the aggregate cartel rate $C(\sigma)$.

Having derived the steady-state set of cartels for a given value for σ, we can define the mass of cartel cases generated by the CLP. If $\theta < \sigma$, then leniency is sufficiently generous relative to non-leniency enforcement that, on cartel collapse, all firms race for leniency. The mass of leniency cases is then

$$L(\sigma) = \int_{\underline{\eta}}^{\overline{\eta}} [1 - H(\phi^*(\sigma, \eta))]C(\sigma, \eta)G'(\eta)d\eta.$$

If $\sigma \leq \theta$, then it is not optimal to apply for leniency, so $L(\sigma) = 0$. The mass of cartel cases generated without use of the CLP is

$$R(\sigma) = qr(C(\sigma) - L(\sigma))$$

$$= \begin{cases} qrC(\sigma), & \text{if } \sigma \leq \theta \\ qr \int_{\underline{\eta}}^{\overline{\eta}} H(\phi^*(\sigma, \eta))C(\sigma, \eta)G'(\eta)d\eta & \text{if } \theta < \sigma \end{cases}.$$

If the CLP is never used (that is, when $\sigma \leq \theta$), then the mass of cases being handled by the CA is $qrC(\sigma)$. If instead $\theta < \sigma$, so that dying cartels use the CLP, then the cartels left to be caught are those that have not collapsed in the current period, which is $\int_{\underline{\eta}}^{\overline{\eta}} H(\phi^*(\sigma, \eta))C(\sigma, \eta)G'(\eta)d\eta$.

- Step 3: Given $C(\sigma)$, solve for the equilibrium value of σ, denoted by σ^*. The probability that the CA's investigation is successful, $v(\lambda L + R)$, depends on the caseload, which depends on how many cartels there are, which depends on σ. Hence, σ^* is a fixed point: $\sigma^* = qrv[\lambda L(\sigma^*) + R(\sigma^*)]$. Having derived σ^*, the equilibrium cartel rate is $C(\sigma^*)$.

As a first step in describing results, consider how a CLP affects the cartel rate $C(\sigma)$ holding non-leniency enforcement fixed. Let us compare the cartel rate with no leniency, denoted $C_{NL}(\sigma)$, with that for full leniency ($\theta = 1$), denoted $C_L(\sigma)$. Under fairly general conditions, it is shown that $C_{NL}(\sigma) > C_L(\sigma)$. Hence, for any level of non-leniency enforcement σ, the cartel rate is lower with a CLP. The reasoning is similar to that described in section 4.5.2.

When non-leniency enforcement is endogenized, the central question posed is: Can a CLP be counterproductive and actually raise the cartel rate? And, if so, what complementary policies make it more likely that a CLP has the desired effect of reducing the frequency of cartels? When penalties are not too severe (i.e., γ is low, where the penalty equals γ times the incremental value from colluding) and the resources saved by prosecuting a leniency case are not large enough (specifically, $\lambda > qr$), then the introduction of a CLP raises the cartel rate. To understand the forces that drive this result, first note that a CLP can affect the cartel rate by disabling active cartels (that is, shutting them down) and by deterring new cartels from forming. A CLP can have a perverse effect because, while it generally promotes deterrence, it can actually result in fewer cartels being shut down.

Prior to the introduction of a CLP, the CA is discovering, prosecuting, and convicting cartels by using non-leniency means. While some of the cartels that are convicted will just so happen to have internally collapsed, many of them will have been active, in which case it is their prosecution and conviction that shuts the cartel down. When a CLP is introduced, cartels that collapse result in its members applying for leniency, and these leniency applications make up part of the caseload of the CA. Of particular note is that leniency cases are coming from dying cartels, and thus prosecution of them is not shutting down active cartels. These leniency cases add to the CA's caseload and thereby result in reduced success in prosecuting non-leniency cases, which, if such a case had led to a conviction, would have disabled a well-functioning cartel. In essence, leniency cases (which do not shut down an active cartel) are crowding out non-leniency cases (which often do shut down active cartels). If leniency cases do not save much in terms of prosecutorial resources (i.e., λ is not sufficiently less than one), then this crowding-out effect is significant and the result is that fewer cartels are shut down when there is a CLP. This is not the end of the story, however. Due to the CLP, a dying cartel is now assured of paying penalties, because one of its members will enter the CLP and aid the CA in obtaining a conviction. In contrast, without a CLP, only a fraction of those cartels would have been discovered and penalized. Thus, a CLP raises the expected penalties for a cartel in the event of its death, which serves to deter some cartels from forming. However, if penalties are not large enough (i.e., γ is not sufficiently great), then the additional cartels deterred due to a CLP is small in comparison to the reduction in the number of cartels shut down because leniency cases crowd out non-leniency cases. As a result, on net, the cartel rate is higher. Thus, in spite of the CLP apparently "working" in the sense of bringing forth leniency applications, it is actually counterproductive in that the latent cartel rate is higher.

Another useful finding related to this perverse effect is that a CLP has a differential effect across industries. The introduction of a CLP can result in *longer* duration for the most stable cartels (i.e., when η is low), while shutting down or shortening the duration of the least stable cartels (i.e., when η is high). To understand what is driving the differential effect of a CLP across industries, recall that only dying cartels use the CLP. Once market conditions are such that collusion is no longer incentive compatible, firms stop colluding and race to apply for leniency. Because the CLP then ensures conviction when the cartel dies, expected penalties are higher. At the same time, the flow of leniency applications can weaken non-leniency enforcement by reducing the likelihood of being prosecuted and convicted outside the CLP. In sum, expected penalties can be higher through the CLP, while lower outside the CLP. Which of these effects is more important depends on an industry's type. Firms in markets that support relatively unstable cartels know there is a significant chance that the cartel will internally collapse and thereby induce a race for leniency. Those cartels are especially harmed by the higher penalties coming from a CLP, and therefore they are worse off. In contrast, firms in markets that support relatively stable cartels are less concerned with a race for leniency, because cartel collapse is unlikely. The greater concern for a highly stable cartel is non-leniency enforcement, and if that is weaker by virtue of the crowding-out effect of a CLP, expected penalties are actually lower; therefore, the environment is more hospitable for collusion.

Sufficient conditions are also provided in Harrington and Chang (2015) for a CLP to have the intended effect of lowering the cartel rate. If penalties are high (i.e., γ is high) and leniency cases are handled expeditiously so that they save sufficient resources (i.e., λ is low), then a CLP will lower the cartel rate. More severe penalties enhance the deterrence effect associated with paying penalties upon cartel collapse, which can offset fewer cartels being shut down. If fewer resources are needed to handle a leniency case, less crowding out of non-leniency enforcement occurs, which can even result in non-leniency enforcement being stronger when there is a CLP.

4.5.4 Multimarket Collusion
Some special issues arise regarding the impact and design of leniency programs when colluding firms supply multiple markets, which is a rather typical occurrence. One such instance is when

product manufacturers form a cartel that operates in different geographic markets (for example, a global cartel selling in different countries). As is known by Bernheim and Whinston (1990), multimarket contact can promote collusion by linking collusion in a market with a binding equilibrium condition with collusion in a market with a nonbinding equilibrium condition. Doing so allows more collusion in the former market while not lessening the extent of collusion in the latter market. When those markets are in different jurisdictions with their own leniency programs, Choi and Gerlach (2012a) show that the impact of a leniency program on the equilibrium conditions is reduced for similar reasons. When firms do not link markets, suppose that the only equilibrium always has firms apply for leniency in the event of an investigation. If they link markets then, in the event that an investigation is opened in both jurisdictions, equilibrium can now have firms applying for leniency in only one market. The potential benefits from CAs sharing information is then explored. While sharing information that contributes to opening an investigation (or to convicting in the event of an investigation) makes collusion more difficult, sharing information about leniency applicants is not always beneficial. If a firm that applies for leniency in one jurisdiction knows it will lead to its prosecution in a second jurisdiction, then the choice becomes applying to both or none. If non-leniency enforcement is moderately low, then firms will choose to apply to neither jurisdiction, while if the CAs did not share confidential information about leniency applicants, then firms would have applied for leniency in one of the markets. In that instance, the efficacy of leniency programs is reduced, though for other cases it can be enhanced.[16]

Collusion in multiple markets can also arise when firms participate in cartels in different product markets, such as the vitamins cartel, which encompassed more than a dozen products. Such a setting is explored in Marshall, Marx, and Mezzetti (2015), which focuses on a particular feature of the CLP in the United States known as Penalty Plus. If, during an investigation of collusion in one market, a firm fails to reveal its participation in other cartels and the other cartels are subsequently discovered, then firms lose (or might lose) the right to apply for leniency in those cartels. Penalty Plus is shown to possibly reduce the likelihood of conviction in currently unsuspected cartels. The intuition is as follows. Suppose that currently an investigation is being conducted in market I. Under Penalty Plus, firms are asked to reveal any other cartels they are involved with. At that moment, the likelihood that the CA would discover and convict them in the other cartels may be sufficiently low that firms decline to reveal them. Given that the Penalty Plus feature prevents them later using leniency in the event of an investigation in the other market, the CLP is now impotent for the cartels that are thus far undiscovered. Hence, an investigation in market I reduces the likelihood of conviction for the cartel in market II. There is, however, a compensating effect, which is that Penalty Plus can make firms more inclined to use leniency in market I.

Building on this insight, Marshall, Marx, and Mezzetti (2015) argue that firms can strategically game the CLP. Consider a situation in which firms primarily want to collude in market I. They may then collude in some minor market II, apply for leniency there, and not report their collusion in market I. In that way, the CLP is neutralized with respect to market I, which serves to make collusion more stable there. The model leaves out a critical factor, however, which is investigation spillovers. The probability that there will be an investigation in market I is *higher* by virtue of firms colluding in market II because of "cartel profiling," whereby the Antitrust Division "will target its proactive efforts in industries where we suspect cartel activity in adjacent markets or which involve one or more common players from other cartels." [17]

Another feature of the U.S. CLP pertinent to multimarket cartels is Amnesty Plus. If a firm did not receive leniency for colluding in market I and then reports its involvement in market II, it receives leniency in market II and a fine reduction in market I. Lefouili and Roux (2012) explore some implications of Amnesty Plus using an extensive form that is a modification of the one in Chen and Rey (2013). When firms colluded in both markets and did not apply for leniency in those markets, there is a probability of conviction in each of the markets. Amnesty Plus is relevant in the event that conviction occurs in, say, market I but not in market II. In that situation, firms simultaneously decide whether to apply for leniency in market II. If a firm receives leniency, it pays no penalty for having colluded in market II and has a reduction in its penalty in market I of an amount R.[18] Amnesty Plus is shown to have two countervailing effects on collusion. As probably intended, it reduces cartel duration for the second undiscovered cartel, because it enhances the financial incentive to apply for leniency. However, it has a deleterious effect, which is that Amnesty Plus weakens deterrence—and, more specifically, encourages multimarket collusion—because expected profit is higher from a strategy of colluding and self-reporting other cartels after an initial conviction. Amnesty Plus is then productive in disabling existing cartels but counterproductive in deterring cartels from forming.

4.5.5   Eligibility and Other Issues

One of the more contentious dimensions to CLPs concerns eligibility and whether instigators (or ringleaders)[19] and recidivists[20] should be prohibited from receiving leniency. The issue of instigator eligibility is examined in Chen, Ghosh, and Ross (2015). The extensive form begins with two firms simultaneously deciding whether to instigate a cartel. If neither instigates, then there is no cartel. If one firm instigates, then the other firm decides whether to agree; if it does, then a cartel is formed. (If both choose to instigate, then one of them is randomly selected as the instigator.) In the event of forming a cartel, each firm decides whether to set the collusive price (in the context of the Prisoners' Dilemma). The CA randomly starts an investigation, and then firms simultaneously decide whether to apply for leniency. Risk dominance is used as an equilibrium selection device, which implies that a firm's calculus includes the prospect that the other firm will apply for leniency (even though firms do not do so in equilibrium). The analysis identifies a trade-off that results from putting in place a no immunity for instigator clause. If, say, firm 1 was the instigator, then it cannot apply. In this case, firm 2's incentive to apply weakens, which makes collusion more stable. In contrast, a no immunity clause reduces the incentive to be an instigator, which reduces the likelihood of an equilibrium in which a cartel forms. There is also an interesting pro-collusion effect when firms are asymmetric. If the firm with the more stringent equilibrium condition is made the instigator, then its inability to apply for leniency weakens its incentive to deviate, which serves to stabilize collusion.

Related to the issue of eligibility, Sauvagnat (2014) considers making leniency contingent on how many firms apply for it. Under the U.S. Department of Justice's Corporate Leniency Program, a necessary condition for an applicant to qualify for leniency when an investigation has already started is that the Division lacks evidence against the company that is likely to lead to a conviction. Motivated by that type of condition, there is research into the minimum amount of delivered evidence needed to be awarded leniency.[21] Some research examines how a CLP affects the incentives to retain evidence and conceal the cartel, for example, through the use of third-party facilitators.[22] Related to that issue (though not dealing with a CLP), Reuter (2013) considers making the fine sensitive to whether cartelists used a third party, such as a trade association, to assist them in colluding. Motivated by the expanding use of private enforcement, Buccirossi, Marvão, and Spagnolo (2015) explore the effect of a CLP when firms are liable for damages but damages are not covered by leniency.

4.6   Summary of Findings

The insights that can be derived from research on the optimal design of competition policy are rather limited, which is partly due to the lack of research but also to the restrictions placed on the dimensions of competition policy. If the CA's decision to pursue a case depends on economic data (specifically, prices and quantities), then optimal enforcement has the CA tolerate low levels of collusion to more effectively deter high levels as well as to save on enforcement costs. With regard to the formula for penalties, the socially optimal design departs from that used by all jurisdictions. The penalty should not condition on revenue nor on incremental profit but rather on the overcharge. Specifically, it should be the overcharge multiplied by the but-for quantity (i.e., the amount that would have been sold at the competitive price), which differs from how customer damages are calculated (which uses the actual quantity sold and thus is determined by the collusive price).

Some subtle implications have been derived for when the penalty is customer damages. When customers are aware of the presence of a cartel and anticipate the possibility of collecting damages, buyers may be no better off than if there were no penalties. The prospect of receiving compensation for each unit purchased causes buyers to have more price-inelastic demand, which induces the cartel to price higher. When firms are colluding with respect to an intermediate good and only direct buyers have legal standing to be compensated, the cartel can induce those buyers not to sue by sharing the rents with them. Furthermore, this can be done in a way that does not legally implicate buyers: the cartel restricts supply below demand (at the collusive price), which raises the final product price received by direct buyers. Finally, it was shown that a standard method for estimating damages using post-cartel data can induce firms to price above the competitive level in the post-cartel environment. Such strategic pricing causes an overestimate of the but-for price, which lowers estimated damages.

The policy issue for which theoretical research has been most extensive is leniency programs. This research has identified a number of key forces that determine how a leniency program influences cartel behavior. The prosecution effect captures the incentive to apply for leniency out of concern that the CA will detect the cartel and levy full penalties. The preemption effect is the incentive to apply before another cartel member does. These two effects are complementary in that a higher prosecution effect encourages a firm (and its rivals) to apply, which, through the preemption effect, further heightens the incentive to apply. Turning to its impact on cartel stability, a program that offers more leniency can enhance the incentive to deviate, as a firm can simultaneously undercut price and avoid penalties by receiving leniency (the Deviator Amnesty Effect). While collusion is then made less stable, more leniency has a complicated influence on cartel stability through its effect on the value to colluding by affecting expected penalties. More leniency directly reduces expected penalties, as the leniency awardee pays less (the Cartel Amnesty Effect) but raises expected penalties by shifting the post-cartel equilibrium from all firms not applying to all firms applying for leniency (Race to the Courthouse Effect). On net, these three effects generally make collusion more difficult when a leniency program is more generous.

Regarding the optimal properties of a leniency program, this body of work largely (though not exclusively) recommends (1) granting maximal leniency for the first firm to come forward prior to an investigation, (2) allowing for leniency even after an investigation has started (though probably only partial leniency), and (3) not limiting eligibility for ringleaders and recidivists. As exemplified by Amnesty Plus, there can be a tension between providing incentives to shut down active cartels and deterring cartels from forming. Furthermore, some features may be vulnerable to gaming by colluding firms, as shown for Penalty Plus. Finally, without the proper setting of complementary instruments, a leniency program may not only be ineffective but actually detrimental. It could result in more cartels, because it weakens non-leniency enforcement. Avoiding that outcome requires setting penalties sufficiently high and putting in place a process that reduces the burden on the CA when handling leniency cases.

5   Some Areas for Future Research

In conclusion, I suggest some areas in need of theoretical research. Arguably the key missing element from models of cartels is the managers who are actually colluding. The presumption in most research is that a manager acts in the best interests of shareholders by taking full account of the additional profits delivered by forming a cartel as well as the possible corporate penalties that may be imposed. Of course, agency issues are always present, and the interests of managers and shareholders do not coincide. This may result in too little collusion from the perspective of shareholders, because managers are not the residual claimants of profits and could open themselves up to penalties in the form of dismissal, debarment, government fines, and even incarceration. At the same time, there could be situations in which managers collude too much. If penalties are severe enough, collusion may be unprofitable, yet managers collude because their performance is improved due to higher division profit—for which they are rewarded with bonuses and promotion—while their superiors are unaware of the latent liability associated with possible conviction and corporate penalties. The theory of collusion needs to be enriched with the managerial dimension and, once that is done, there are competition policy issues to pursue regarding individual versus corporate penalties and programs that might enhance the conflict of interest between managers and shareholders.[1]

Career concerns are also relevant when considering the behavior of a competition authority. The models of a CA considered in chapter 4 generally assume it would act in a manner to maximize social welfare. Presumably, members of a CA are instead interested in maximizing their perceived performance while taking into account any personal costs. As the impact of policies and actions on social welfare is difficult to assess (especially since the population of cartels in the economy is not directly observable) is it not at all clear whether it is even possible to design incentive schemes to induce CA members to care about social welfare. For example, the head of a CA might believe his or her income and future job prospects are most impacted by how many cartels are prosecuted, how many cases are won, and how much in fines is collected. A CA may then put more weight on shutting down cartels than on deterring cartels from forming—as the former is more observable than the latter— and may avoid difficult cases (though the pursuit of them could enhance deterrence). Given a reasonable representation of a CA member taking account of career concerns, one can explore how a CA's behavior may depart from that which is socially optimal and how the proper use of rules and discretion may lead to better welfare outcomes.[2]

Some research has been done but much more is needed on using theory to help measure the impact of competition policy. A new competition policy—such as a leniency program—should be considered effective if it reduces the number of cartels (as well as saves resources in the enforcement of competition laws). The fundamental data challenge is that we do not observe the population of cartels; rather, only discovered cartels are observed. Changes in the number of discovered cartels need not proxy for changes in the number of cartels. For example, if the number of discovered cartels declines after the adoption of a policy, is it because there are fewer cartels or because the likelihood of discovery is lower? Furthermore, the population of discovered cartels need not be a representative sample of the population of cartels, so changes in properties of discovered cartels (such as duration) need not reflect the characteristics of all cartels.[3] Theory can be useful for identifying possible biases and how one might use observable data—such as discovered cartels—to infer what is going on with the latent population of cartels. For example, Harrington and Chang (2009) show how a change in the duration of discovered cartels can be a measure of the efficacy of a new policy. Drawing on ecological methods for measuring animal populations in the wild, Ormosi (2014) uses recidivism to measure the latent cartel rate.[4] It is not enough to devise and implement new policies to fight cartels. It is critical that we figure out how to measure the impact of those polices—are they working?—and theory could prove useful (if not essential) in light of the data challenges.

The process by which colluding firms pay penalties involves detection, prosecution, and conviction. Thus far, research has generally been sparse in modeling those stages. It is typical to conflate them into a single probability, which misses out on many relevant enforcement issues. In practice, judicial and administrative processes generally do not allow purely economic evidence to determine guilt in a cartel case out of concern of wrongly convicting firms that are not colluding. And then there are the false negatives, whereby colluding firms are either not detected, are suspected but not prosecuted (perhaps due to lack of evidence, lack of resources, or the career concerns of CA members that lead them to pass on tough cases), or are prosecuted but not convicted. Expanding the definition of liability (e.g., so it includes more forms of tacit collusion) and lowering the evidentiary standards (e.g., allowing economic evidence to be sufficient) could chill competition, while narrowing and raising standards would encourage cartel formation and allow collusion to continue unabated. Kaplow (2013) provides an excellent discussion of this trade-off, but there is a conspicuous lack of formal models addressing these issues. Models need to factor in various legal regimes and how illegality depends on the manner in which firms collude and not just on whether they collude.

It means modeling meetings among cartel members to coordinate and share information, and determining how it impacts the efficacy of collusion and the evidence that is produced. The integration of liability and evidentiary standards in economic models of collusion is a vast unexplored territory. Until we venture into it, a fundamental question in the area of competition law and enforcement will remain open: What is the socially optimal definition of unlawful collusion?

Appendix: Notation

δ is the discount factor.

n is the number of firms.

$\pi(p)$ is a firm's profit when all firms charge a common price.

$\pi^d(p)$ is a firm's profit when it chooses a price to maximize current profit given that all other firms are charging p.

π^c is a firm's profit when firms collude.

π^n is a firm's profit at a static Nash equilibrium.

V^n is a firm's value when firms compete.

V^c is a firm's value when firms collude.

σ is the probability of paying penalties.

ω is the probability of an investigation.

ρ is the probability of conviction conditional on an investigation.

f is the current period's fine, and F is the cumulative fine.

x is the current period's penalty, and X is the cumulative penalty.

γ is the penalty multiple applied to some base to generate the total penalty.

ζ is the probability of the cartel reforming in the period after a conviction.

$1 - \beta$ is the depreciation rate of the cumulative penalty.

Notes

Preface

1. United States v. Topco Assocs., 405 U.S. 596, 610, n. 10 (1972).

1 Introduction

1. For coverage of the general theory of collusion in the repeated game framework, some useful references are Tirole (1988), Vives (1999), and Motta (2004).

2. "Every contract, combination in the form of trust or otherwise, or conspiracy, in restraint of trade or commerce among the several States, or with foreign nations, is declared to be illegal."

3. American Tobacco Co. v. United States, 328 U.S. 781 (1946).

4. Monsanto Co. v. Spray-Rite Serv., 465 U.S. 752 (1984).

5. Judgment of the Court of July 15, 1970. ACF Chemiefarma NV v. Commission of the European Communities, Case 41–69.

6. Judgment of the Court of First Instance of October 26, 2000. Bayer AG v. Commission of the European Communities.

7. Werden (2004, 770, 779)

8. Clamp-All Corp. v. Cast Iron Soil Pipe, 851 F.2d at 484 (1st Cir. 1988).

9. Baker (1993, 179)

10. Kovacic (1993, 19)

11. Page (2009, 451)

12. Brooke Group Ltd. v. Brown & Williamson Tobacco Corp., 509 U.S. 209 (1993).

13. For a discussion of excessive pricing laws, see Evans and Padilla (2005).

14. For some discussion of this last point, see Harrington (2013b).

15. Some collusive theories have communication as *part of an equilibrium* (which are briefly discussed in section 3.3.3) and, depending on what is conveyed, that could be sufficient for illegality. Here, I am referring to communication *to reach an equilibrium*, which is the primary (though not exclusive) focus of the law.

16. Equilibrium theories are *not* theories of how firms can collude without communication. It is a non sequitur to say that assuming mutual beliefs in a game without communication shows how firms can achieve mutual beliefs without communication (and thus how firms can collude without communication).

17. If an economist thinks there is substance to referring to collusion as "tacit," then what is an example of "explicit collusion" in economic theory? Some might say it is when collusion can be enforced through binding contracts, but that is an irrelevant category that runs contrary to law and practice. Collusive arrangements have never been enforceable in most countries and, to my knowledge, currently are enforceable in none.

18. For a review of some experimental work, see Choi and Gerlach (2015); for empirical work, see Levenstein and Suslow (2006, 2015).

19. Papers of which I am aware are Aubert, Rey, and Kovacic (2006); Angelucci and Han (2011); and Thêpot and Thêpot (2016).

20. For example, Jullien and Rey (2007).

3 Impact of Competition Policy on Collusion

1. The ensuing analysis is from Harrington (2014).

2. It is straightforward to adapt the ensuing analysis to allow the cartel to reform with some probability. Also, one could allow σ to vary over time; see Hinloopen (2006).

3. It is immediate that $\Psi(\sigma, f, \beta)$ is increasing in f and β. A sufficient condition for $\Psi(\sigma, f, \beta)$ to be increasing in σ is $\sigma \leq 1/2$ which is a necessary condition for collusion to be stable; that is, if $\sigma > 1/2$ then (3.4) does not hold.

4. For example, Selten (1973), Prokop (1999), and Kuipers and Olaizola (2008).

5. For some progress on this topic, see Paha (2013).

6. One can get "collapse" (in the sense that there are no collusive equilibria) with the Bertrand price game but, essentially, it is a special case of the Prisoners' Dilemma, where $\pi^d = n\pi^c$ and $\pi^n = 0$.

7. Examples can be found in Harrington (2006), Connor (2008), and Marshall and Marx (2012).

8. Also see Bartolini and Zazzaro (2011) and Kalb (2016).

9. For a theoretical and empirical analysis of collusive pricing dynamics due to uncertainty about cartel stability, see Chilet (2016).

10. Having enriched the setting beyond the Prisoners' Dilemma, there are then many continuation equilibria associated with a deviation. For simplicity, I focus on the grim punishment, though the results to be discussed are generally robust to the equilibrium selection.

11. One way to motivate low markups is to augment the model so that there is a perfect substitute for this good outside this market that sells for $\tilde{p} > p^n$. This implies the collusive price cannot exceed $\tilde{p}$ (for if it did, then all consumers would turn to buying the substitute good). For markets in which $\tilde{p}$ is close to p^n, the collusive price will be $\tilde{p}$ and the markup will be low.

12. Of course, this is an expectation, so that an illegal cartel would not form if the markup was expected to be small. If there is uncertainty about what markup is stable, then the realized markup could be small.

13. There is a related finding in Jensen and Sørgard (2014), where it is shown that penalties tend to cause the incentive compatibility constraint (determining the collusive price) to bind for cartels able to produce large overcharges, and for the participation constraint (determining whether collusion is profitable) to bind for cartels only able to produce low overcharges.

14. Chen and Harrington (2007) and Bos, Peeters, and Pot (2013) also show how competition policy can have perverse effects by promoting collusive behavior.

15. For an early paper on the dynamics of collusive pricing when there is the threat of prosecution, see Levy and Rodriguez (1987).

16. The ensuing analysis is based on Harrington (2003, 2004a, 2005).

17. In equilibrium, all firms charge the same price, so the summary statistic is that common price.

18. As the noncollusive price path is an affine function of cost, it also shows how cost is moving over time.

19. A discussion of this theory and other research in the context of screening for cartels is provided in Harrington (2007, 2008a).

20. For the model of Athey and Bagwell (2001), Hörner and Jamison (2007) show how almost first-best payoffs can be achieved without communication. That paper speaks to the statement made earlier that there are many clever and complicated ways to effectively collude without sending messages.

21. Also see Escobar and Llanes (2016), which shows the value of communication about private information on market conditions in the context of collusion.

22. The proof uses a result of Kalai and Lehrer (1993), though it is not subject to the criticism of their "grain of truth" assumption, because, given the other assumptions on firms' prior beliefs, the support is a countable set.

23. Equilibrium without communication was originally characterized in Garrod and Olczak (2016b).

24. It is shown that results are robust to not assuming verifiable information but instead having the price report be cheap talk, in which case an incentive compatibility constraint must be satisfied for it to be truthful. However, the proof of robustness relies heavily on the special assumptions made on demand and capacities.

25. A caveat to that statement is that a cartel may want to keep itself hidden to affect bargaining with industrial buyers. Buyers may be more willing to accept a large price increase if they think it is due to higher cost than to a change in firm conduct; see Kumar et al. (2015) and Kumar (2016).

4 Optimal Competition Policy

1. For the interested reader who would like to wade into the literature on liability and evidentiary standards pertaining to collusion, I recommend (in this order): Kaplow (2013), Werden (2004), Page (2007), Hay (2000), Harrington (2011a), Kovacic et al. (2012), and Coate (2015).

2. It is then important that noncollusion means perfect competition; otherwise there is a first-order negative effect on welfare from reducing supply below the noncollusive level.

3. This result runs counter to that found in Katsoulacos, Motchenkova, and Ulph (2015a), which is reviewed below.

4. Martin (2006) and Frezal (2006) derive optimal competition policy in a dynamic setting, but the set of possible policies is very restrictive. Martin (2006) has firms either compete, lawfully collude (which involves imperfect monitoring in a Green-Porter model), or unlawfully collude (which takes the form of joint profit-maximization). The CA can decide whether to impose a penalty depending on the observed price. Frezal (2006) considers audit policies for which the CA decides whether to investigate an industry. The study finds that timing the auditing of industries in a known deterministic way can be better than random auditing. Intuitively, a probability of auditing (which then would cause cartel termination) may be insufficient to deter collusion in some industries. However, if an industry knew that it would be audited for sure at some future time, then the resulting known terminal date for collusion would, by backward induction, undermine collusion in all periods. While intriguing, both random and deterministic auditing policies are probably impractical.

5. In *Bell Atlantic Corp. v. Twombly*, 550 U.S. 544 (2007), the U.S. Supreme Court stated that, for purposes of pleading a claim, "an allegation of parallel conduct and a bare assertion of conspiracy will not suffice" and that the the plaintiff must present "enough facts to state a claim to relief that is plausible on its face." Thus, a plausibility standard has been erected for a case to proceed. For a discussion of this issue, the reader is referred to Klevorick and Kohler-Hausmann (2012).

6. In the United States, the maximum potential fine is twice the gain to the cartel or the loss to consumers.

7. Other works exploring issues concerning the optimal magnitude and design of penalties include Buccirossi and Spagnolo (2007); Motchenkova (2008); Allain et al. (2011); Bageri, Katsoulacos, and Spagnolo (2013); Katsoulacos and Ulph (2013); Jensen and Sørgard (2014); and Kalb (2016).

8. At the optimal price under customer damages, the derivative equals zero, which then implies that the derivative under the overcharge-based penalty is negative, which implies, by strict concavity, that the cartel wants to set a lower price.

9. From a customer compensation perspective, the overcharged-based formula is also more appropriate, because a penalty is assessed not only on the quantity that is purchased, $D(p)$, but also on the forgone quantity, $D(p^n) - D(p)$, which does not occur under customer damages.

10. Katsoulacos, Motchenkova, and Ulph (2015b, 79)

11. See Verboven and van Dijk (2009), Basso and Ross (2010), and Boone and Müller (2012). Some related work models private litigation in antitrust cases: Briggs, Huryn, and McBride (1996); Bourjade, Rey, and Seabright (2009); and Reuter (2012).

12. This is true at the federal level but about half of the states do allow indirect purchasers to sue.

13. For individual penalties of fines and incarceration, the United States also has an Individual Leniency Program and, in fact, the awarding of corporate leniency typically grants individual leniency to all employees (though there can be carve-outs of some employees). Research has almost exclusively focused on corporate leniency, and that is what is covered here.

14. Park (2014) provides a procurement auction setting with bids from a continuum and shows that the Race to the Courthouse Effect disappears. This result implies that full leniency is always optimal.

15. These steps are described in greater detail in section 3.1.2 in the context of Harrington and Chang (2009).

16. Additional issues related to operating a cartel in multiple geographic markets are explored in Choi and Gerlach (2012b, 2013).

17. Hammond (2004, 15).

18. This is equivalent to providing a reward (in addition to avoiding all penalties) from reporting involvement in a second cartel. While in general, competition authorities are opposed to offering rewards, Amnesty Plus effectively does so.

19. Herre, Mimra, and Rasch (2012); Bos and Wandschneider (2013); and Chen, Ghosh, and Ross (2015).

20. Ishibashi and Shimizu (2010) and Chen and Rey (2013).

21. Harrington (2008b) and Blatter, Emons, and Sticher (2014).

22. Aubert, Rey, and Kovacic (2006) and Marx and Mezzetti (2014).

5   Some Areas for Future Research

1. For some research on collusion with managers, see Spagnolo (1999, 2005).

2. Harrington (2011b) touches on this issue by comparing the socially optimal caseload (which minimizes the cartel rate) with the privately optimal caseload (which is presumed to maximize the number of convictions). If detection and conviction are not too difficult, a CA is not aggressive enough in that it prosecutes too few cases.

3. This point is examined in Harrington and Wei (2015).

4. Also see Davies and Ormosi (2014) and Katsoulacos, Motchenkova, and Ulph (2015b), who offer general frameworks for assessing enforcement.

References

Allain, Marie-Laure, Marcel Boyer, Rachidi Kotchoni, and Jean-Pierre Ponssard. "The Determination of Optimal Fines in Cartel Cases—The Myth of Underdeterrence." CIRANO Working Paper 2011s-34, March 2011.

Angelucci, Charles, and Martijn A. Han. "Private and Public Control of Management." Amsterdam Center for Law & Economics Working Paper 2010-14, July 2011.

Aoyagi, Masaki. "Collusion in Dynamic Bertrand Oligopoly with Correlated Private Signals and Communication." *Journal of Economic Theory* 102 (2002): 229–248.

Athey, Susan, and Kyle Bagwell. "Optimal Collusion with Private Information." *RAND Journal of Economics* 32 (2001): 428–465.

————. "Collusion with Persistent Cost Shocks." *Econometrica* 76 (2008): 493–540.

Aubert, Cecile, Patrick Rey, and William Kovacic. "The Impact of Leniency and Whistle-Blowing Programs on Cartels." *International Journal of Industrial Organization* 24 (2006): 1241–1266.

Awaya, Yu, and Vijay Krishna. "On Communication and Collusion." *American Economic Review* 106 (2016): 285–315.

Bae, Hyung. "A Price-Setting Supergame Between Two Heterogeneous Firms." *European Economic Review* 31 (1987): 1159–1171.

Bageri, Vasiliki, Yannis Katsoulacos, and Giancarlo Spagnolo. "The Distortive Effects of Antitrust Fines Based on Revenue." *Economic Journal* 123 (2013): F545–F557.

Baker, Jonathan B. "Private Information and the Deterrent Effect of Antitrust Damage Remedies." *Journal of Law, Economics, and Organization* 4 (1988): 385–408.

————. "Two Sherman Act Section 1 Dilemmas: Parallel Pricing, the Oligopoly Problem, and Contemporary Economic Theory." *Antitrust Bulletin* 38 (Spring 1993): 143–219.

Bartolini, David, and Alberto Zazzaro. "The Impact of Antitrust Fines on Formation of Collusive Cartels." *B. E. Journal of Economic Analysis & Policy* 11 (2011): 1–28.

Basso, Leonardo J., and Thomas W. Ross. "Measuring the True Harm from Price-Fixing to Both Direct and Indirect Purchasers." *Journal of Industrial Economics* 58 (2010): 895–927.

Bernheim, B. Douglas, and Michael D. Whinston. "Multimarket Contact and Collusive Behavior." *RAND Journal of Economics* 21 (1990): 1–26.

Besanko, David, and Daniel F. Spulber. "Antitrust Enforcement under Asymmetric Information." *Economic Journal* 99 (1989): 408–425.

———. "Are Treble Damages Neutral? Sequential Equilibrium and Private Antitrust Enforcement." *American Economic Review* 80 (1990): 870–887.

Blatter, Marc, Winand Emons, and Silvio Sticher. "Optimal Leniency Programs When Firms Have Cumulative and Asymmetric Evidence." Universität Bern, working paper, July 2014.

Block, Michael K., Frederick C. Nold, and Joseph G. Sidak. "The Deterrent Effect of Antitrust Enforcement." *Journal of Political Economy* 89 (1981): 429–445.

Boone, Jan, and Wieland Müller. "The Distribution of Harm in Price-Fixing Cases." *International Journal of Industrial Organization* 30 (2012): 265–276.

Bos, Iwan, Stephen Davies, Joseph E. Harrington, Jr., and Peter L. Ormosi. "Does Enforcement Deter Cartels? A Tale of Two Tails." University of East Anglia, working paper, September 2016.

Bos, Iwan, and Joseph E. Harrington, Jr. "Endogenous Cartel Formation with Heterogeneous Firms." *RAND Journal of Economics* 41 (2010): 92–117.

———. "Competition Policy and Cartel Size." *International Economic Review* 56 (2015): 133–153.

Bos, Iwan, Ronald Peeters, and Erik Pot. "Do Antitrust Agencies Facilitate Meetings in Smoke-Filled Rooms?" *Applied Economics Letters* 20 (2013): 611–614.

Bos, Iwan, and Frederick Wandschneider. "A Note on Cartel Ringleaders and the Corporate Leniency Program." *Applied Economics Letters* 20 (2013): 1100–1103.

Bourjade, Sylvain, Patrick Rey, and Paul Seabright. "Private Antitrust Enforcement in the Presence of Pre-Trial Bargaining." *Journal of Industrial Economics* 57 (2009): 372–409.

Briggs, Hugh C., III, Kathleen D. Huryn, and Mark E. McBride. "Treble Damages and the Incentive to Sue and Settle." *RAND Journal of Economics* 27 (1996): 770–786.

Buccirossi, Paolo, Catarina Marvão, and Giancarlo Spagnolo. "Leniency and Damages." Stockholm School of Economics, working paper, November 2015.

Buccirossi, Paolo, and Giancarlo Spagnolo. "Optimal Fines in the Era of Whistleblowers: Should Price Fixers Still Go to Prison?" In *The Political Economy of Antitrust*, edited by V. Ghosal and J. Stennek, 81–122. Amsterdam: Elsevier, 2007.

Chan, Jimmy, and Wenzhang Zhang. "Collusion Enforcement with Private Information and Private Monitoring." *Journal of Economic Theory* 157 (2015): 188–211.

Chen, Joe, and Joseph E. Harrington, Jr. "The Impact of the Corporate Leniency Program on Cartel Formation and the Cartel Price Path." In *The Political Economy of Antitrust*, edited by V. Ghosal and J. Stennek, 59–80. Amsterdam: Elsevier, 2007.

Chen, Zhijun, and Patrick Rey. "On the Design of Leniency Programs." *Journal of Law and Economics* 56 (2013): 917–957.

Chen, Zhiqi, Subhadip Ghosh, and Thomas W. Ross. "Denying Leniency to Cartel Instigators: Costs and Benefits." *International Journal of Industrial Organization* 41 (2015): 19–29.

Chilet, Jorge Alé. "Gradually Rebuilding a Relationship: Collusion in Retail Pharmacies in Chile." Hebrew University, working paper, April 2016.

Choi, Jay Pil, and Heiko Gerlach. "Global Cartels, Leniency Programs and International Antitrust Cooperation." *International Journal of Industrial Organization* 30 (2012a): 528–540.

————. "International Antitrust Enforcement and Multimarket Contact." *International Economic Review* 53 (2012b): 635–658.

————. "Multi-Market Collusion with Demand Linkages and Antitrust Enforcement." *Journal of Industrial Economics* 61 (2013): 987–1022.

————. "Cartels and Collusion—Economic Theory and Experimental Evidence." In *Oxford Handbook on International Antitrust Economics*, edited by D. Blair and D. Sokol, 415–441. Oxford: Oxford University Press, 2015.

Coate, Malcom B. "Plus Factors in Price Fixing: Insightful or Anachronistic?" In *Economic and Legal Issues in Competition, Intellectual Property, Bankruptcy, and the Cost of Raising Children*, edited by J. Langenfeld, 1–41. *Research in Law and Economics*, Vol. 27, Bingley, UK: Emerald Group Publishing, 2015.

Connor, John M. *Global Price Fixing*. 2nd ed. Berlin: Springer, 2008.

Cyrenne, Philippe. "On Antitrust Enforcement and the Deterrence of Collusive Behavior." *Review of Industrial Organization* 14 (1999): 257–272.

Davies, Steve, and Peter L. Ormosi. "The Economic Impact of Cartels and Anti-Cartel Enforcement." University of East Anglia, working paper, October 2014.

Ellis, Christopher J., and Wesley W. Wilson. "Cartels, Price-Fixing, and Corporate Leniency Policy: What Doesn't Kill Us Makes Us Stronger." University of Oregon, 2001.

Escobar, Juan, and Gastón Llanes. "Cooperation Dynamics in Repeated Games of Adverse Selection." Universidad de Chile, working paper, November 2016.

Evans, David S., and A. Jorge Padilla. "Excessive Prices: Using Economics to Define Administratable Legal Rules." *Journal of Competition Law and Economics* 1 (2005): 97–122.

Frezal, Sylvestre. "On Optimal Cartel Deterrence Policies." *International Journal of Industrial Organization* 24 (2006): 1231–1240.

Friedman, James W. *Oligopoly and the Theory of Games*. Amsterdam: North-Holland, 1977.

Garrod, Luke, and Matthew Olczak. "Collusion, Firm Numbers and Asymmetries Revisited." Loughborough University, working paper, January 2016a.

————. "Collusion under Imperfect Monitoring with Asymmetric Firms." Loughborough University, March 2016b (*Journal of Industrial Economics*, forthcoming).

Gärtner, Dennis. "Corporate Leniency in a Dynamic World: The Preemptive Push of an Uncertain Future." University of Bonn, working paper, October 2013.

Gerlach, Heiko. "Stochastic Market Sharing, Partial Communication and Collusion." *International Journal of Industrial Organization* 27 (2009): 655–666.

Green, Edward J., and Robert H. Porter. "Noncooperative Collusion under Imperfect Price Information." *Econometrica* 52 (1984): 87–100.

Hammond, Scott D. "Cornerstones of an Effective Leniency Program." ICN Workshop on Leniency Programs, Sydney, Australia, November 22–23, 2004.

Harrington, Joseph E., Jr. "Collusion among Asymmetric Firms: The Case of Different Discount Factors." *International Journal of Industrial Organization* 7 (1989): 289–307.

———. "The Determination of Price and Output Quotas in a Heterogeneous Cartel." *International Economic Review* 32 (1991): 767–792.

———. "Some Implications of Antitrust Laws for Cartel Pricing." *Economics Letters* 79 (2003): 377–383.

———. "Cartel Pricing Dynamics in the Presence of an Antitrust Authority." *RAND Journal of Economics* 35 (2004a): 651–673.

———. "Post-Cartel Pricing During Litigation." *Journal of Industrial Economics* 52 (2004b): 517–533.

———. "Optimal Cartel Pricing in the Presence of an Antitrust Authority." *International Economic Review* 46 (2005): 145–169.

———. "How Do Cartels Operate?" *Foundations and Trends in Microeconomics* 2 (July 2006).

———. "Behavioral Screening and the Detection of Cartels." In *European Competition Law Annual 2006: Enforcement of Prohibition of Cartels*, edited by C.-D. Ehlermann and I. Atanasiu, 51–68. Oxford: Hart Publishing, 2007.

———. "Detecting Cartels." In *Handbook of Antitrust Economics*, edited by P. Buccirossi, 213–258. Cambridge, MA: MIT Press, 2008a.

———. "Optimal Corporate Leniency Programs." *Journal of Industrial Economics* 56 (2008b): 215–246.

———. "Posted Pricing as a Plus Factor." *Journal of Competition Law and Economics* 7 (2011a): 1–35.

———. "When Is an Antitrust Authority Not Aggressive Enough in Fighting Cartels?" *International Journal of Economic Theory* 7 (2011b): 39–50.

———. "Corporate Leniency with Private Information: An Exploratory Example." In *Recent Advances in the Analysis of Competition Policy and Regulation*, edited by J. E. Harrington Jr. and Y. Katsoulakos, 28–48. Cheltenham, UK: Edward Elgar, 2012.

———. "Corporate Leniency Programs When Firms Have Private Information: The Push of Prosecution and the Pull of Pre-emption." *Journal of Industrial Economics* 61 (2013a): 1–27.

———. "Evaluating Mergers for Coordinated Effects and the Role of 'Parallel Accommodating Conduct.'" *Antitrust Law Journal* 78 (2013b): 651–668.

———. "Penalties and the Deterrence of Unlawful Collusion." *Economics Letters* 124 (2014): 33–36.

————. "A Theory of Collusion with Partial Mutual Understanding." *Research in Economics* 71 (2017): 140–158.

Harrington, Joseph E., Jr., and Myong-Hun Chang. "Modelling the Birth and Death of Cartels with an Application to Evaluating Antitrust Policy." *Journal of the European Economic Association* 7 (2009): 1400–1435.

————. "When Should We Expect a Corporate Leniency Program to Result in Fewer Cartels?" *Journal of Law and Economics* 28 (2015): 417–449.

Harrington, Joseph E., Jr., and Joe Chen. "Cartel Pricing Dynamics with Cost Variability and Endogenous Buyer Detection." *International Journal of Industrial Organization* 24 (2006): 1185–1212.

Harrington, Joseph E., Jr., and Andrzej Skrzypacz. "Private Monitoring and Communication in Cartels: Explaining Recent Collusive Practices." *American Economic Review* 101 (2011): 2425–2449.

Harrington, Joseph E., Jr., and Yanhao Wei. "What Can the Duration of Discovered Cartels Tell Us about the Duration of All Cartels?" University of Pennsylvania, The Wharton School, December 2015 (*Economic Journal*, forthcoming).

Hay, George A. "The Meaning of 'Agreement' under the Sherman Act: Thoughts from the 'Facilitating Practices' Experience." *Review of Industrial Organization* 16 (2000): 113–129.

Herre, Jesko, Wanda Mimra, and Alexander Rasch. "Excluding Ringleaders from Leniency Programs." University of Cologne, working paper, April 2012.

Hinloopen, Jeroen. "Internal Cartel Stability with Time-Dependent Detection Probabilities." *International Journal of Industrial Organization* 24 (2006): 1213–1229.

Hörner, Johannes, and Julian Jamison. "Collusion with (Almost) No Information." *RAND Journal of Economics* 38 (2007): 804–822.

Houba, Harold, Evgenia Motchenkova, and Quan Wen. "Competitive Prices as Optimal Cartel Prices." *Economics Letters* 114 (2012): 39–42.

Ishibashi, Ikuo, and Daisuke Shimizu. "Collusive Behavior under a Leniency Program." *Journal of Economics* 101 (2010): 169–183.

Jensen, Sissel, and Lar Sørgard. "Fine Schedule with Heterogeneous Cartels: Are the Wrong Cartels Deterred?" Norwegian School of Economics, working paper, March 2014.

Jullien, Bruno, and Patrick Rey. "Resale Price Maintenance and Collusion." *RAND Journal of Economics* 38 (2007): 983–1001.

Kalai, Ehud, and Ehud Lehrer. "Rational Learning Leads to Nash Equilibrium." *Econometrica* 561 (1993): 1019–1045.

Kalb, Jonas. "The Effect of Penalty Regimes on Endogenous Cartel Formation." University of St. Andrews, working paper, March 2016.

Kaplow, Louis. *Competition Policy and Price Fixing.* Princeton, NJ: Princeton University Press, 2013.

Katsoulacos, Yannis, Evgenia Motchenkova, and David Ulph. "Measuring the Effectiveness of Anti-Cartel Interventions: A Conceptual Framework." University of St. Andrews, working paper, December 2015a.

————. "Penalizing Cartels: The Case for Basing Penalties on Price Overcharge." *International Journal of Industrial Organization* 42 (2015b): 70–80.

Katsoulacos, Yannis, and David Ulph. "Antitrust Penalties and the Implications of Empirical Evidence on Cartel Overcharges." *Economic Journal* 123 (2013): F558–F581.

Klevorick, Alvin K., and Issa B. Kohler-Hausmann. "The Plausibility of Twombly: Proving Horizontal Agreements after Twombly." In *Research Handbook on the Economics of Antitrust Law*, edited by Einer R. Elhauge, 201–245. Cheltenham, UK: Edward Elgar, 2012.

Kovacic, William E. "The Identification and Proof of Horizontal Agreements under the Antitrust Laws." *Antitrust Bulletin* 38 (1993): 5–81.

Kovacic, William E., Robert C. Marshall, Leslie M. Marx, and Halbert L. White. "Plus Factors and Agreement in Antitrust Law." *Michigan Law Review* 110 (2012): 393–436.

Kuipers, J., and N. Olaizola. "A Dynamic Approach to Cartel Formation." *International Journal of Game Theory* 37 (2008): 397–408.

Kumar, Vikram. "Collusive Price Announcements with Strategic Buyers." Chicago: Compass Lexecon, October 2016.

Kumar, Vikram, Robert C. Marshall, Leslie M. Marx, and Lily Samkharadze. "Buyer Resistance for Cartel versus Merger." *International Journal of Industrial Organization* 39 (2015): 71–80.

LaCasse, Chantale. "Bid Rigging and the Threat of Government Prosecution." *RAND Journal of Economics* 26 (1995): 398–417.

Lefouili, Yassine, and Catherine Roux. "Leniency Programs for Multimarket Firms: The Effect of Amnesty Plus on Cartel Formation." *International Journal of Industrial Organization* 30 (2012): 624–640.

Levenstein, Margaret C., and Valerie Y. Suslow. "What Determines Cartel Success?" *Journal of Economic Literature* 44 (2006): 43–95.

————. "Cartels and Collusion—Empirical Evidence." In *Oxford Handbook on International Antitrust Economics*. Vol. 2, edited by D. Blair and D. Sokol, 442–463. Oxford: Oxford University Press, 2015.

Levy, David, and Alvaro Rodriguez. "Does the Threat of Antitrust Policy Keep Prices Down? or: Making Hay While the Sun Shines." *International Journal of Industrial Organization* 5 (1987): 341–350.

Marshall, Robert C., and Leslie M. Marx. *The Economics of Collusion—Cartels and Bidding Rings*. Cambridge, MA: MIT Press, 2012.

Marshall, Robert C., Leslie M. Marx, and Claudio Mezzetti. "Antitrust Leniency with Multi-Product Colluders." *American Economic Journal: Microeconomics* 7 (2015): 205–240.

Martin, Stephen. "Competition Policy, Collusion, and Tacit Collusion." *International Journal of Industrial Organization* 24 (2006): 1299–1332.

Marx, Leslie M., and Claudio Mezzetti. "Effects of Antitrust Leniency on Concealment Effort by Colluding Firms." *Journal of Antitrust Enforcement* 2 (2014): 305–332.

McCutcheon, Barbara. "Do Meetings in Smoke-Filled Rooms Facilitate Collusion?" *Journal of Political Economy* 105 (1997): 330–350.

Motchenkova, Evgenia. "Determination of Optimal Penalties for Antitrust Violations in a Dynamic Setting." *European Journal of Operational Research* 189 (2008): 269–291.

Motta, Massimo. *Competition Policy: Theory and Practice.* Cambridge: Cambridge University Press, 2004.

Motta, Massimo, and Michele Polo. "Leniency Programs and Cartel Prosecution." *International Journal of Industrial Organization* 21 (2003): 347–379.

Mouraviev, Igor. "Explicit Collusion under Antitrust Enforcement." Bielefeld University, working paper, August 2013.

Ormosi, Peter L. "A Tip of the Iceberg? The Probability of Catching Cartels." *Journal of Applied Econometrics* 29 (2014): 549–566.

Page, William H. "Communication and Concerted Action." *Loyola University Chicago Law Journal* 38 (2007): 405–460.

———. "*Twombly* and Communication: The Emerging Definition of Concerted Action under the New Pleading Standards." *Journal of Competition Law and Economics* 5 (2009): 439–468.

Paha, Johannes. "Cartel Formation with Endogenous Capacity and Demand Uncertainty." MAGKS Discussion Paper Series 43-2013, September 2013 (*Journal of Industrial Economics*, forthcoming).

Park, Sangwon. "The Effect of Leniency Programs on Endogenous Collusion." *Economics Letters* 122 (2014): 326–330.

Porter, Robert H. "Optimal Cartel Trigger Price Strategies." *Journal of Economic Theory* 29 (1983): 313–338.

Prokop, Jacek. "Process of Dominant-Cartel Formation." *International Journal of Industrial Organization* 17 (1999): 241–257.

Reuter, Tim. "Private Antitrust Enforcement Revisited: The Role of Private Incentives to Report Evidence to the Antitrust Authority." University of Konstanz Working Paper 2012-04, February 2012.

———. "Endogenous Cartel Organization and Antitrust Fine Discrimination." University of Konstanz Working Paper 2013-09, May 2013.

Rotemberg, Julio J., and Garth Saloner. "A Supergame-Theoretic Model of Price Wars During Booms." *American Economic Review* 76 (1986): 390–407.

Salant, Stephen W. "Treble Damage Awards in Private Lawsuits for Price Fixing." *Journal of Political Economy* 95 (1987): 1326–1336.

Sauvagnat, Julien. "Are Leniency Programs Too Generous?" *Economics Letters* 123 (2014): 323–326.

———. "Prosecution and Leniency Programs: The Role of Bluffing in Opening Investigations." *Journal of Industrial Economics* 63 (2015): 313–338.

Schinkel, Maarten Pieter, and Jan Tuinstra. "Imperfect Competition Law Enforcement." *International Journal of Industrial Organization* 24 (2006): 1267–1297.

Schinkel, Maarten Pieter, Jan Tuinstra, and Jakob Rüggeberg. "Illinois Walls: How Barring Indirect Purchaser Suits Facilitates Collusion." *RAND Journal of Economics* 39 (2008): 683–698.

Schmalensee, Richard. "Competitive Advantage and Collusive Optima." *International Journal of Industrial Organization* 5 (1987): 351–367.

Selten, Reinhard. "A Simple Model of Imperfect Competition, Where 4 Are Few and 6 Are Many." *International Journal of Game Theory* 2 (1973): 141–201.

Silbye, Frederik. *Topics in Competition Policy: Cartels, Leniency, and Price Discrimination.* PhD thesis, University of Copenhagen, August 2010.

Souam, Saïd. "Optimal Antitrust Policy under Different Regimes of Fines." *International Journal of Industrial Organization* 19 (2001): 1–26.

Spagnolo, Giancarlo. "On Interdependent Supergames: Multimarket Contact, Concavity, and Collusion." *Journal of Economic Theory* 89 (1999): 127–139.

———. *Divide et Impera*: Optimal Deterrence Mechanisms against Cartels and Organized Crime." University of Mannheim, working paper, 2003.

———. "Managerial Incentives and Collusive Behavior." *European Economic Review* 49 (2005): 1501–1523.

———. "Leniency and Whistleblowers in Antitrust." In *Handbook of Antitrust Economics*, edited by Paolo Buccirossi, 259–303. Cambridge, MA: MIT Press, 2008.

Spector, David. "Facilitating Collusion by Exchanging Non-verifiable Sales Reports." Paris School of Economics, working paper, February 2015.

TFEU (Treaty on the Functioning of the European Union). 1999.

Thêpot, Florence, and Jacques Thêpot. "Collusion, Executive Compensation, and Antitrust Fines." University of Glasgow, working paper, June 2016.

Tirole, Jean. *The Theory of Industrial Organization.* Cambridge, MA: MIT Press, 1988.

Verboven, Frank, and Theon van Dijk. "Cartel Damage Claims and the Passing-On Defense." *Journal of Industrial Economics* 57 (2009): 457–491.

Vives, Xavier. *Oligopoly Pricing: Old Ideas and New Tools.* Cambridge, MA: MIT Press, 1999.

Werden, Gregory J. "Economic Evidence on the Existence of Collusion: Reconciling Antitrust Law with Oligopoly Theory." *Antitrust Law Journal* 3 (2004): 719–800.

Yao, Dennis A., and Susan S. DeSanti. "Game Theory and the Legal Analysis of Tacit Collusion." *Antitrust Bulletin* 38 (Spring 1993): 113–141.

Index